Jason Allday

Cover Artwork: Ben Marsh

ISBN-13: 9798594855557
Cover Design: Ben Marsh

Rule Britannia

"When Britain first, at Heaven's command

Arose from out the azure main;

This was the charter of the land,

And guardian angels sang this strain:

"Rule, Britannia! rule the waves:

"Britons never will be slaves."

In 1763 James Thompson published those words that, (couldn't have better) encapsulated the might and pride of a small island located off the north shores of main-land Europe.

A song that most 1970's and '80's British school children would sing at one time or another during morning assembly. Patriotism and a sense of our national identity was taught throughout the United Kingdom; whether it be from within the household or your schooling, a very sense of our national identity was ingrained within us all from an early age.

The Brits. So, who are we?

I once read an article on what is perceived as the 'traditional brit' and their Idiocrasies. From this article, I could only assume their source was a failed script on the history of jolly old. A more accurate representation would be to either speak with people that have invested a considerable amount of time in, or are actually born and raised from the U.K. So, it remains and it's fair to say, depending on who you ask, their experience on dealing with the tea drinking, crumpet eating, eccentric royal leaning islanders, but will typically give you a different (some-what humorous, but equally accurate) reply.

Some of my more favourite examples given to me on 'us weird lot' include, but not limited to what a typical Brit is - polite, condescending, arrogant, traditionalist, cynical, liberal, eccentric, conservative, poor cooks, reserved, complacent, stuffy, tolerant, humorous, modest, class conscious, all football (soccer) fans are hooligans to name but a few.

A few common traits

Oi! There's a queue!

It's been said we do love a queue. We really have perfected the art for queuing up. So much so that we've set a world standard and passion for queuing up for anything. Not hard to understand our level of patience really when we wait all year for a spot of good weather.

A cuppa'.

Of all that you might hear and read, Brits are not alcoholics, or do we raise our children on pints of warm ale and binge drink for seven days a week at the local pub. But if we are to be defined by one stereo typical ideal, it's going to be we're a nation of tea drinkers. One thing we are not only experts on, but we're world leaders on making a decent cup of tea. The fact we don't believe in contaminating it with additives or extras such as lemon or herbs, "just milk and sugar if you please, sir!" The British recipe for any national disaster, whether it's economical, a power outage during a Christmas special of a favourite tv sitcom or natural disaster, all problems and issues are solved by making a 'nice cup of tea'. Tea is drunk at almost any time with an estimated consumption measured in the hundreds of millions of cups daily.

To live and survive (more harmoniously) in the UK, for most, is to maintain a sense of humour and treat life with contempt when it, (life) tries to take the piss. Our philosophy is a simple one: you have to deal with much of life with a simple approach, especially when we're an island surrounded by water and are on a year-round government-imposed hose-pipe ban. A friend once said to me, "you lot built an Empire with a Bible in one hand, and a musket in the other". How far from the truth is that!

By now, most would agree, unless you've been secluded from any true cultural exposure and are educated enough to know that there's no such thing as a 'typical Brit' and very few people conform to what is believed to be a standard British chap.

'Britishness' - heads held high

So, you might ask, why such a strong sense of national identity from such a small island? Could it be a need to belong, a need for security, stability and a sense of identity?

It's been written that Britishness is said to be the state, or quality of being British, or of embodying British characteristics. It comprises the claimed qualities that bind and distinguish the British people and form the basis of their identity, and the ideals of British culture. Examples could be our habits, behaviours, or symbols, that have a common, familiar or iconic quality readily identifiable with the United Kingdom. It's also a belief and with a level resources of imagination and shared symbolism that's found within all hard-working fellow Englishman, that also contributes to the Britishness, that is identified with for those not only born and raised within the harbouring green shores, but those that assimilate and align with traditions found within.

Some would of course argue that anyone claiming their country is the best and has a high level of patriotism, probably hasn't travelled anywhere outside of their own country. There may be some truth to that statement, as an interesting article on nationalism and pride was reported on when a survey taken and shown in the British newspaper, The Telegraph, showed Indonesia and India have some of the most patriotic people and claiming a very high percentage (over 80%) of the population said they are very proud of their nationality. Accepting that both India and Indonesia are poor countries and a very small percentage of the population actually have a passport and simply down to economic status, are unable to travel, again could lend some credit to the original argument of 'not traveling' But, something that needs to be considered is the British are quite the common and well versed of global travellers. With a high percentage of the population having a passport, now promotes a different theory. Why is a populace that's experienced and well versed in international travel, still proud of their iconic and shows a high level of nationalism? Could this suggest there's less justification in the opening statement?

A fact most will agree on, is the promise and great benefit for the prospective traveller, who owns a passport and 'puts one foot in front of the other', as travel allows them to enhance their development skills, teaches a person to be adaptable to changing situations and be more flexible. All elements of travel are healthy key components to a person's growth.

Something that should be noted is the unique benefit and key aspect to the wide verse of cultural investment and exposure that London has. London is one of the most culturally diverse cities in the world. This is attributed to the once great reach of the British Royal Navy, the early docking years of trade and commerce that would come largely and solely into London via the river Thames and of course our documented historical sea faring days of past. A country that is experienced and versed in international travel, and still proud of their iconic level of nationalism. It Could be said, "quite an achievement"

There's a similar level of cultural and social identity found within our close cousins across the pond; the septic's, who also show a very strong shared belief, in terms of morals and a standard for a healthy life style, all be it both considered somewhat idealistic, but all the same a healthy and happy life - after all, Britain and America have long since held one of the strongest and most powerful diplomatic relationships in the modern world.

Conclusion?

If I was to generalise, I think as a collective nation, it has something to do with the English having a developed world view and knowledge of history that makes us aware of how lucky we are to have been born, raised and live in a country that recognises a person's rights and ability to speak as much for, as against people's rights and the democracy we all live in.

So, on a more individual level, what makes someone with such a strong sense of national identity leave such a great nation? It could be said, being that inherently found within a sea faring island race, is that sense or yearning to seek 'higher grounds', so to speak. Or to wander to pastures greener? Or could it be simply ones wish to escape the confines and restrictions of such a reserved and conservative post Victorian upbringing? It could be answered by those that do have the luxury of traveling and living overseas, upon returning home, a favourable common phrase and statement made is, "it's nice to be home" My conclusion, is that there isn't anyone reason why one would leave, but as I have learned over the years, there are many reasons I simply enjoy coming home.

Welcome, one and all!

What Could be one of the many reasons international travellers would want to visit the United Kingdom? London has reportedly been one of the most visited cities in the world. Not forgetting, of course our other great neighbouring cities throughout the UK.

Could it be our Extensive and Fascinating History? Or could it be our vibrant culture shown in many of our museums and cities around the country? Or as many have said, the scenery!

In addition to the United Kingdom offering some of the best scenery in the entire world, don't be fooled by the stereo typical belief that the food isn't that great. While it's true that British food is often commented on as being bland, what it may lack in saveur and flair will over- compensate with originality and a meaningful back story. When I'm hard pressed for an intellectual response to someone complaining on them having to try English food and who's also hell bent on seeking some justification on why they have to eat that 'boring food', I'll treat such a question and comment with contempt and reply, "What's wrong with a diet of fish, chips, biscuits and tea, anyway?"

In London, as well as a number of other cities across the UK, you will find some of the best restaurants. And the truth being the UK also has some of the most eccentric and best chefs in the world.

So, food could be a reason in itself! Now I'm not to compete with our septic cousins, but sports, as many people in the United Kingdom testify, we definitely take our sports seriously. Funnily enough, it was recently commented on a popular tv show that, "The British are sports mad, although most people confine their interest to watching or gambling rather than taking part."

A Week Away

The Kebab – Vinnie Stone

The Sunday Roast – Scott Peden

Football – Irvine Welsh

Pie n Mash – Ricky Grover

The British Café – Carlton Leach

I'm popping back home!

So, why come back (for my holiday?)

As many ex pats have experienced, living in another country changes you forever. You will never be the same and will never be afforded the same routine and rituals. One of the most common customs a lot of us Brits make when traveling abroad is looking for the same old, same old creature comforts we're accustomed to. The pub, a full English, a copy of the worst that Fleet Street has to offer and the people around us. Visiting, (amongst other continents) the European Mediterranean and her bounty of countries of both warmth and history should promote the healthy human instinct of enrichment in new sights and sounds within us all. Instead, a good few indulge in the same comforts as if they were on a day out down to Brighton - you know the sort, your typical group of lads, all sporting their new outfits with an over confident spring in their step, their girlfriends entow, all google eyed and romanticising about their chosen potential head-of-house hold leading the pack. And of course, not forgetting the ever so known, cultural rhetoric of the teenage and early twenties youth shouting, "More beer, Pedro!" Admit it, we were all there once.

So for those that have been lucky, or simply worked hard enough for the benefit of a dual nationality, why come home? From the many conversations with mates that have also taken to moving overseas, who sought a sense of adventure and traded in their stone island jumpers for the timeless classics of polo shirts and Adidas gazelles, and speaking from my own personal experience, the shared answer is a simple one - there's no place like home!

For the many people that have been given the opportunity to ventures new and embracing a different lifestyle, will tell you that level of appreciation and respect, (or they should!) when moving to another country. In many cases, a warmer climate, advancement in both economic and personal growth, and of course the chance for a pool in your own back garden should be invitation even for the biggest of pessimists.

A well-documented article I once read said It is true, we are familiar with things where we live, eat and sleep. We also know the streets and which sides of them to drive on. We typically know what type of food we like to eat, and we also follow habitual routines. Many of our daily actions are done without even thinking about them. We know the people who we live and work with. We know the patterns and how we communicate with others around us. We know the 'cracks in the ceiling and the 'creaks in the floor'. We may not pay conscious attention to all of these little details, but we identify and are accustomed to them. These same customs, routines and communications are a sense of security and comfort for many, after all, for many years we have created our very own identity through these same routines and practices. But, as many will also tell you, for all of the excitement and unnerving level of positive emotions of packing a case and leaving pastures green, there's something you have to sacrifice - and that's your level of social and cultural identity.

One of the hardest things to accept when leaving the most iconic city in the world, is no longer having the privilege to say, "I live in London!", as there's nothing that can never equal that sense of pride or feeling (later commonly referred to as culture shock). For all her faults, issues and challenges, the feeling gained from saying you're from London, was on par with wearing that saying as a badge of honour. The memories of childhood antics, family who once played a role in your growing up, the mates you'd call upon, no matter the weather or time of day, the corner shop you'd all hang outside as your local meeting place. The locally owned chip shop that gave you an extra portion of chips at no charge, as your family had been regulars and friends with the owners since the day you could crawl. The luxury of being able to walk past the same bus stop you kissed a girl for the first time while waiting for the bus to take her home, and the same bus stop she dumped you at, only then to drive off on the back of some wankers motorbike. You're conscientiously and willingly abandoning and giving up all the countless memories, sacrifices and experiences you have with that place you once called home. So, why leave - wouldn't you if given the chance? The same conflicts and anguish many have faced and probably asked themselves, for me have become an easy one to answer and cure - "Fuck it! Let's go home for a week". This become a common phrase I would throw around the household when I felt the need for a little 'cultural fix!'. Change is inevitable, the very face and look of the old neighbourhood will have changed, but the moral fabric of your old community will not. That you carry with you, as no amount of over-bearing, classless, mis shaped modern car parks and chain driven shopping centres will ever change who you are and what you value. The chip shop owners may have since long retired and moved on, the corner shop that once stood as the focal point for the local council estate kids to hear and find out all that was new was forced to close and make way for a new multi shopping centre, the same girl that dumped you, came to her senses some years later and said, "yes!", (once you'd dropped the ego and your pride), and the mates you had as a kid, for the most are still knocking about, and as much of all of those are but memories, it's still a place you can still always come back to and call home.

History Can be Fun

So, Big Ben, the Cotswolds and the White Cliffs of Dover. What else is known about jolly old?

It was once said, In the late 19th century, a South London plumber named Thomas Crapper manufactured one of the first widely successful lines of flush toilets with a ballcock, a tank-filling mechanism still used today. Hence a toilet being called a "Crapper". And that ain't no Crap!

It gets worse!

People used to use urine to tan animal skins, so families used to all pee in a pot & then once a day it was taken & Sold to the tannery; if you had to do this to survive you were "Piss Poor"

But worse than that were the really poor folk who couldn't even afford to buy a pot; they "didn't have a pot to piss in" and were deemed the lowest of the low

The next time you are washing your hands and complain because the water temperature isn't just how you like it, think about how things used to be.

Here are some facts about the 1500's.

Most people got married in June because they took their yearly bath in May, and they still smelled pretty good by June. However, since they were starting to smell, brides carried a bouquet of flowers to hide the body odor. Hence the custom today of carrying a bouquet when getting Married.

Baths consisted of a big tub filled with hot water. The man of the house had the privilege of the nice clean water, then all the other sons and men, then the women and finally the children. Last of all the babies. By then the water was so dirty you could actually lose someone in it. Hence the saying, "Don't throw the baby out with the bath water!"

Houses had thatched roofs-thick straw-piled high, with no wood underneath. It was the only place for animals to get warm, so all the cats and other small animals (mice, rats etc) lived in the roof. When it rained it became slippery and sometimes the animals would slip and fall off the roof. Hence the saying "It's raining cats and dogs."

There was nothing to stop things from falling into the house. This posed a real problem in the bedroom where bugs and other droppings could mess up your nice clean bed. Hence, a bed with big posts and a sheet hung over the top afforded some protection. That's how canopy beds came into existence.

The floor was dirt. Only the wealthy had something other than dirt. Hence the saying, "Dirt poor." The wealthy had slate floors that would get slippery in the winter when wet, so they spread thresh (straw) on floor to help keep their footing. As the winter wore on, they added more thresh until, when you opened the door, it would all start slipping outside. A piece of wood was placed in the entrance way. Hence: a thresh hold.

In those old days, they cooked in the kitchen with a big kettle that always hung over the fire. Every day they lit the fire and added things to the pot. They ate mostly vegetables and did not get much meat. They would eat the stew for dinner, leaving leftovers in the pot to get cold overnight and then start over the next day. Sometimes stew had food in it that had been there for quite a while. Hence the rhyme: Peas porridge hot, peas porridge cold, peas porridge in the pot nine days old. Sometimes they could obtain pork, which made them feel quite special. When visitors came over, they would hang up their bacon to show off.

It was a sign of wealth that a man could, "bring home the bacon." They would cut off a little to share with guests and would all sit around and chew the fat.

Those with money had plates made of pewter. Food with high acid content caused some of the lead to leach onto the food, causing lead poisoning death. This happened most often with tomatoes, so for the next 400 years or so, tomatoes were considered poisonous.

Bread was divided according to status. Workers got the burnt bottom of the loaf, the family got the middle, and guests got the top, or the upper crust.

Lead cups were used to drink ale or whisky. The combination would Sometimes knock the imbibers out for a couple of days. Someone walking along the road would take them for dead and prepare them for burial. They were laid out on the kitchen table for a couple of days and the family would gather around and eat and drink and wait and see if they would wake up. Hence the custom of holding a wake.

England is old and small and the local folks started running out of places to bury people. So they would dig up coffins and would take the bones to a bone-house, and reuse the grave. When reopening these coffins, 1 out of 25 coffins were found to have scratch marks on the inside and they realized they had been burying people alive... So they would tie a string on the wrist of the corpse, lead it through the coffin and up through the ground and tie it to a bell. Someone would have to sit out in the graveyard all night (the graveyard shift.) to listen for the bell; thus, someone could be, saved by the bell or was considered a dead ringer.

And that's the truth. Now, whoever said History was boring!

The Black Cab

Without question, the London taxi is one of the most recognisable symbols and travel institutes of London life. If you've not had the opportunity to go to London, there's a good chance you've seen one in the thousands of movies, millions of newspapers and photographs reflecting London and its inhabitants.

The London taxi, officially known as Hackney carriages or cabs for hire, the most common version of history says the taxi got their start on the streets of London in the 1600's. Also, a heavily agreed upon historical story suggests they got their name from the French word hacquenee, that stood for small horse for hire. The original Hackneys were compact one horse two wheeled carriages that were small and mobile enough to navigate the busy narrow streets.

Locals and users of the carriages of the time often referred to them as 'hackney hell carts', due to the drivers being reckless and the carts themselves kept unclean and unsanitary.

It has been written that London's first cab rank for the carriages was situated on The Strand. The pioneer was a captain, John Bailey, a veteran of one of Sir Walter Raleigh's expeditions. From 1634 he managed a rank of four horse drawn carriages, available for hire from The Strand. Bailey's cab men wore a distinctive uniform, would charge customer a fixed tariff depending on distance. The cab profession was given an official approval and 1654 when one of the first acts of parliament and Oliver Cromwell set up the fellowship of Master Hackney carriages. This brought the trade under the control of a quart of aldermen in the city of London. By the middle 1700s there we're over 1,000 licensed taxis navigating the busy town of London.

Wilhelm Bruhn invented the taximeter in 1891, and it is from the word taxi meter that taxi became the new byword for the cab. The taxi meter measured the distance, as well as the time, is taken for an accurate fare of the journey to be charged. The word comes from French taxe ('price') and Greek metron ('measure'). Some stories suggest the London taxi drivers of the time did not like being told by a machine how much to charge, but whatever their disdained opinion on the added mechanism, the term taxi meter become the standard reference for taxis worldwide.

The first motorized taxis were introduced in the early 1900's, but the classic line of London cabs didn't make its symbolism until the introduction of the Austin SXT model. This model had the characteristic silhouette and came with an orange roof sign. This iconic model is the reason why today's trademark colour of the London taxi is black. The manufacture was producing the vehicle as black by default and buyers had to pay extra if they wanted any other colour. For a while, the cars were being purchased by fleet owners in batches, and so as to stay within budget lines, nobody wanted to pay extra for something as non-essential as a different colour. Another interesting detail, to date all black cabs have to be tall enough to accommodate a passenger wearing a bowler hat. There's another story shared between some drivers, going back to 1831, where it's said Hackney carriages held a law that each vehicle had to carry a bail of hay in their boots. It's also said this law was still held even after the motorised cabs were introduced.

Today London cabs can come in any colour, but they are still referred to as black cabs. There's been an attempt to modernise and change the appearance of the cult classic design over the last few decades. The FX3 and FX4 models remained a popular favourite with both consumer and taxi driver. The Austin TX4 is a favourite in current London, as it still shows similar characteristics to earlier models. Another favourite with cabdrivers is the ability of the vehicle being able to turn in very tight quarters - it has a turning circle of just 25 feet, which earned the vehicles common phrase, being able to turn on a two-pence.

The cab design is not the only unique attribute to the quality of a London taxi. Becoming a licensed London taxi, the driver needs to pass the test, commonly known as 'the knowledge'. The special test requires memorising a staggering 25,000 streets, almost as many landmarks and 320 routes, without the assistance of a gps/ satnav or map, and not just limited to names and places, as the examiner can and typically does ask for the applicant to show the most efficient route between two (A and B) points in London by memory. Not to mention a criminal background check and the applicants driving history will also be reviewed. The knowledge covers a 6-mile radius of Charing Cross.

Those that do pass the test are quickly coined, 'butterboys'. Another institutional tradition is if you are lucky enough to get a ride with somebody that has just passed that test, that ride is free. As of 2017, the FX4 was ceased in production. Soon to be replaced by the TX5, thankfully showing some of the tradition and iconic style of their predecessors.

A strange but true law, it is technically breaking the law to shout 'taxi' at a moving black cab. Also, thankfully, a law that is not reinforced, a bizarre black cab law allows the driver to relieve himself, if required, against the rear of the vehicle. The law grants permission as long as the driver's right hand is touching the cab.

The Cab Ride

Brian Anderson

After over 20 years of photographing the UK's most dangerous gangland figures for my newspaper assignments back in the mid '90s, I had decided to tell the story behind some of the pictures for the first time, some of the most dangerous criminals in crimes bloody history, and the story behind the picture of Britain's Godfather Freddie Foreman.

A journey that would see me start in Glasgow probably in the mid '90s, then London, Birmingham, Newcastle, Liverpool, Leeds, Essex, and Dublin and Spain. Guns were pulled out on me, death threats were issued but, all I wanted to do was document history and in the end, trust was earned.

The picture and story I want to talk about is with none other than Freddie Foreman - one of the most notorious names in criminal history that many would agree. As a hitman for the notorious Kray brothers, Freddie was one of the most feared ever, and if you crossed him there would be a good chance you wouldn't ever be seen again and would be become a memory, just trust me on that.

After a bit of lunch on my second visit to see Fred, I ended up in the Punchbowl in Mayfair owned by Guy Ritchie. Once Fred had seen my photos, he was up for anything really, as he realised what I was trying to do. We got on really well and are friends to this day.

Once Fred went to the toilet, I jumped over and paid for lunch, as I didn't want to give the Scots a bad name, he thought that was funny.

We spoke about a lot of stuff and ended up on the subject of movies and crime movies in general. Of course, we ended up talking about the classic film, The Long Good Friday, and if you haven't seen it, then get it as soon as possible, it's one of the best British crime films of all time.

The film was directed by John Mackenzie and starred the great late Bob Hoskins as London gangland figure Harold Shand, which ironically was said to be based on Fred.

Something just clicked and I asked Fred if anyone had ever taken his picture on the Thames with the famous Tower Bridge Backdrop, he said, "no", so we both jumped into a taxi. Here the adventure and comedy begins. As we're on route, it couldn't be missed or ignored, that the cab driver was consistently looking back in his rear-view mirror. As anyone will attest, when you're driving through one of the busiest cities in the world, you need eyes forward at all times. Without question, your traditional black London cabs are nothing short of pure orgasmic when it comes to quality and service. But, something seemed 'odd' and very shifty with the driver. There was something very unsettling, or was is it simply my paranoia? After all, I'm in good hands. I'm riding alongside the godfather of crime. The man who's so heavily respected, it goes without saying, he's a known face and top of the criminal fraternity tree. After a lot of sudden stops and constant eyeballing, we arrive at our destination. Now, the normal routine is for the passengers to get out and meet the driver at the door, pay his way and carry on with their agenda. But, this fella, was 'Johnny on the spot' - jumping out, getting the door and there like lightening to meet us with at minimum a 'look' on his face. There was something inside me that said there's something wrong and amiss. This had all the qualities and makings of a professional hit. A questionable set of actions as a result of his unsettling looks and the 'meet and greet' by the driver upon us getting to our destination. It was only his next set of words that added a level of humour to the scenario, that even to this day I have to laugh over. His nervous stammer and excitement could be heard when the driver simply asked, " is....is... is.... that Freddie Foreman?" I think I need to stop watching all the gangster films, as a simple handshake and request of a photo off the main man was what it all came down to.

Fred himself has since said it was the best picture of him ever taken, he had been pictured by the legendary fashion photographer David Bailey in the 1960s, so it was a pretty cool thing to hear as I was a huge fan of Bailey and his swinging '60s pictures. This and the black cab ride helped solidify a very impressionable and memorable time with One of the last of the old school and The Godfather of crime.

Full English

It was once written, 'you should have breakfast at least three times a day'. The English breakfast, commonly referred to as 'a fry-up', has its referenced historical start up back in the 13th or 14th century, making it arguably one of the most traditional English of dishes.

Looking back at the means and ways of simple survival, a big breakfast was deemed more of a luxury, being the economy dictated a meal was a means of survival more than a way to start your day. So, a big breakfast was simply reserved for the rich and those of great economic means. Your everyday 'working class', if it was afforded, would have nothing more than a bowl of porridge type substance; sometimes the meal would extend to include a piece of bread and ale. Those that had a slight step up on the economic scale of things, would also been rewarded with some cheese, cold meats and or dripping.

The English breakfast is mentioned in certain historical documents in the midst of the 13th century, in the homes of the wealthy and prominent members of the English upper class. The more typical successful and wealthiest classes could be found across different parts of the country, more so in the south of England and also within what is now known as the English countryside. Those within this economic circle, were known as the 'English gentry', who were made up of a self-proclaimed epicentre and leaders of the cultural leaders and founders of everything Anglo Saxon, and a true English lifestyle. The upper class and paymasters would also promote they were to be used as a measure and benchmark, who were to be respected and referenced to as the best of British. It is also worth mentioning fasting before church in Britain and the 'breaking' of that 'fast' afterwards created the British tradition of breakfast which later evolved into the full breakfast.

The upper class were known for their expensive and lavish breakfasts, often employing more than their regular staff so as to impress and out do fellow aristocrats when it came to their breakfast feasts. Some would say this extensive breakfast feast was a way to simply accommodate family, friends and passers-by, but such a lavish start to the day must've required some planning and stocking of foods, but for whatever reason, the breakfast in these circles of this time was no small doing.

A big breakfast was for the same economic circles meant to serve as a means to cover you until your next meal. So, a rigorous day of hunting or a long carriage journey, assumingly would've been made a lot easier after a large meal.

With a change in the economy, the social class divide, was made smaller by a drastic change in the economy. So, the English elite would soon find themselves sharing the spoils of fine foods and ales with industrialists, businessmen, merchants and bankers. Not to totally destroy their social standing and egos, the upper-class elites would hold their status and their breakfast serving size over their staff and the working class.

What remained as a test of time was that the breakfast and all that went along with it was its importance as a meal and a gathering for those wishing to show their ability to provide a hearty and meaningful meal to start the day.

In the Victorian era, breakfast was shown to be an elegant affair. With reason to dress up and parade both yourself and those you held in high regard around to be seen and noted, here again breakfast was nothing short as a means to display not only was you part of a social class but that you had a level of civility that could be shown not only at main banquets and evening events but also at the start of the day; as they say, "once a gentleman always a gentleman".

The Edwardian era allowed the splendour and luxury of the upper class and its close economic cousin the upper middle class to continue with their display of appreciation of fine foods and gatherings that the British empire could boast. This was of course shortly before the First World War, that allowed the British breakfast to be officially marked within the history books as a permanent standard and cornerstone of the great British empire. Also a time when the fry up would start to be included as a common site and option for many traveling around the country and frequenting overnight inns and keeps; known today as bed and breakfasts. It was at this time that the middle class also had access to more affordable foods, employing the same types of foods as a staple input to a family's dietary start to their day.

From here everything was all go and by the late 1940's and early '50's the full English spread to the working class. There's some conflict amongst food experts and historians over the breadth of the population and how many could afford such a meal consisting of meats and quality of food, one fact remains consistent - those that would've typically seen a lot less, now had access and an opportunity to this type of meal, it was recognised as a 'national' dish and was accessible by all social and economic classes.

What become as traditional as the breakfast was the small but often overcrowded greasy spoon type cafes. Often found within working class communities and work areas, the cafes would be bustling with your working class and often seen mixing with the masses, the middle class, who all be could afford a better seat at many a department store type restaurant, would favour the working class environment, not so much for the conversation, but as seen, a 'healthier' and more 'bountiful' serving of breakfast. Industrial work sites and roadside cafes would become as common a sight as the postman and double decker bus.

What remains open for debate, is what the full English breakfast consists of. As much an opinion as an argument, is based typically down to what is served due to geographical location of the served breakfast. Bacon, eggs, toast and eggs remain consistent, but also backed pudding, fried bread, fried tomatoes, backed beans and fried mushrooms. But whatever your chosen breakfast consists of is down to the person placing the order. A change or addition did become clearly evident and that's with the introduction of coffee to the English breakfast table. Tea was always considered part of the 'deal'.

A Full English

Carlton Leach

Aah, the smell of a full English and the (best) person and place that holds that memory is my dad, in the kitchen, cooking up a full plate of what was nothing less than pure heaven. Living in a two up, two down in Forest Gate, you really couldn't ask for a better setting. I can still picture and remember it like it was yesterday. Most weekends I'd be lying in bed as a kid, the smell would just waft up into my room, the smell of bacon and all the trimmings - top drawer! That undeniable smell making its way up to my room. I don't care how late you went to bed the night before, but when that distinctive smell caught your nostrils, it would wake up every taste bud you had, and you'd be up like a shot. Those that remember the old Bisto advert and the kids raising their heads as the smell caught their noses, that helps describe the action. Yeah, that smell was enough to lift me out of my bed, getting dressed and running down the stairs into the kitchen. Always bacon, eggs, sausages, and beans, oh and always tomatoes - yeah, fresh tomatoes, none of that canned rubbish. Dad always did it right. I remember the smells as much as I can my actions. It was that simple action of me jumping up in bed and thinking, 'fuck! Great! Breakfast!', my dad, him cooking a full English, that invokes great memories even to this day. There was no other way I would want to start my day than with dad and a full English. It was such a distinctive smell and anyone that had that experience will vouch for that. And it's bacon, it's always the main ingredient. It's the smell of bacon that does it, it's that smell that pulls you in and that makes a full English breakfast. I know people that eat wisely and healthy, but there's been many a time when they've got that smell of bacon and they've gone weak at the knees, caved and had a full English. It was a tradition as much as it was a ritual. No different than grabbing a copy of the daily newspaper on the way to work, as it was switching on the telly on a Saturday afternoon to get the football results. Thinking about it, if only there was a way I could turn the clock back. And that's my memory of a full English and the value it holds.

The Pub

There's without question nothing more iconic than the British local pub. But why do they exist in the first place? It could be said it can't be answered without concrete evidence or confidence, and some would say it's complicated, as the truth spans over 1,000 years of British history.

The history of the pub, or public house as it was once and accurately known, tells the story of one of England's most unique institutions. Public (houses) places where people could gather and drink date back at minimum to the occupation of the Romans, who first took the basic concept of the pub to Britain in 43 AD. In Rome, it was said landlords would hang branches of vine leaves outside their premises to indicate the trade that was practiced within. However, with vines not exactly in bloom in old Britain, they hung any type of foliage closely resembling a vine plant over the door - there are pubs in the UK called the Bush or Holly Bush to this day.

The Romans built an extensive road network and with their large armies moving around the country, roadside inns opened at specific stopping points. Some modern roads still follow the routes of these ancient highways, so it's entirely possible that some inns have been on the same site ever since the Roman occupation.

But it's worth considering, pubs or drinking houses were first thought to have become a common sight in the Anglo-Saxon period, when people opened their private homes as drinking houses. The Ye Olde Fighting Cocks in St Albans, Hertfordshire, one of several pubs that claim to be the oldest drinking house in England, had open doors that date back to the 8th century.

By the 12th century, people were traveling the country visiting cathedral towns on pilgrimage, such as to the shrine of Thomas Beckett in Canterbury. Chaucer's pilgrims in the Canterbury Tales, began their journey at the Tabard, a real inn located in London. Other inns and taverns catered to pilgrims and knights on their way to the Crusades in the Holy Land. Ye Olde Trip to Jerusalem, established in 1189, claims to be the oldest inn pub in England and has cellars which are carved from the rocks beneath Nottingham Castle.

The Pub is an historical part of English life, and even with in recent years, and the increase in the price of a night out to your local, many true blooded English men still commit to a time old tradition of a pint with his mates.

Throughout all of the world and in all societies, places where people can have a drink together on neutral territory is, and remains part of human nature. Pubs are places where people go to talk to each other, to gossip and catch up on news from near and far. Different continents and countries have their own cultural iconic places of 'worship', the English - and the British Isles in general - their pubs. The English pub has been subjected to sociological surveys, that have shown that the pub is the only place where the English will openly and willingly begin a conversation with a stranger! A study on the very subject makes a strong claim that goes against the controversial UK drinking guidelines, saying that moderate alcohol intake has strong physical and mental health benefits. And who are we to argue with science?

Every traditional pub is distinguished on the outside by its painted pub sign, indicating and illustrating its name. In ye days of olde, illustrated pub signs were vital in order to identify pubs in an age when literacy was lacking in mainstream society. The earliest uses of pub, inn and tavern names would reference the sign directly. People would arrange to meet at the sign of the Crowne and Anchor, more than, I'll meet you at the Crowne and Anchor public house or inn.

The origins of the names of pubs in England are sometimes obscure, typically identifying and relating the pub or inn to a specific alignment with a political or historical event in time. Pubs called The Kings Arms are often to be found in cities or villages which were on the royalist side during the Civil War in the 17th century. Pubs named The Crown, likely adopted the name in relief after

King Charles resumed the throne (and pub activities) after it was seized by Oliver Cromwell in London, the name of the famous pub, The Elephant and Castle is a misinterpretation of The Infanta of Castile, who was the wife of King Edward the 1st. With a few modern exceptions, every pub name can tell either part of the pub's history or its past.

Of course, there are also many gentrified/ modern pubs, especially in city centres, serving a very different and more transient clientele, such as office-workers, tourists, or young people simply out for a jolly up. These are far from your traditional type pubs, simply, they're not respected as they have no character or history, are treated with contempt due to the chain owners lack of aligning or identifying with the pubs heritage and ancestral roots. There are even dictionaries giving an insight into pub names to help you decipher the meanings behind those decorative, ornate and strange-seeming character signs, the savvy historians study pub signs for pointers about the early consumer culture and social customs once found and respected within.

There's been a few credible and accepted studies done on the pub in modern day society. Such research has shown that face-to-face meetings are vital to maintaining friendships, the beneficial role that pubs have in a person's life, and the same studies show that people who use local pubs near where they live or work tend to have more close friends, provide a strong social network that improves happiness and overall health. Even with social networking, enabling people to connect with people all over the world, making and maintaining friendships is something that has to be done face-to-face; the digital world is simply no substitute.

The pub in today's society is still, and will always be a place, where a moderate alcohol intake improves well-being and some (though not all) social skills, just as it has been shown to improve other cognitive abilities and health, but you have to civil qualities decline as alcohol intake increases beyond a moderate level - be smart, as no one likes a loud-mouth!

Today, the modern-day pubs are still the headquarters where alcohol is consumed and mates are met. A lot of pubs also serve meals, have wi-fi, and in-house entertainment. The pub culture dictates that there are, invariably, locals. Locals who have looked down more insides of an empty pint class, than you have seen different managers come and go from your high street chain restaurant. These same locals usually live, work and are a stone's throw to the pub and frequent it, often sticking to the same beer and routine as when they first visited with his dad or older brother many years before. Today, little in reality has changed. There may now be rather fewer pubs in relation to the population and many certainly look rather different from the saw dusted, wooden floor boarded tap rooms of old, but as both time and the regular has shown over the decades, the pub retains its unique position in British society, and for much the same reasons as in days of past, the pub is the only kind of public building used by large numbers of ordinary working class people where their thoughts and actions are not being in some way or another dictated to them; in the other kinds of public building they are the nothing more than member of an audience, watchers of political, athletic events and gatherings. And it's within the same four walls of a pub, once a man has bought or been bought his glass of beer, he has entered an environment in which he is a participator rather than a spectator. Here, you can have your own platform.

The whole idea of human participation in a pub is crucial to understanding what pubs are, and how their unique structure and locals in particular, are all about — even in the digital age of online communities, texting and other forms of instant communication are why people are attracted to pubs and why they commit their focus for social networking. The answer is given, by most, by the following statement - we go to the pub for a drink, we don't go drinking at the pub. Because, by having a drink (rather than just drinking) is essentially a social act surrounded by unspoken rules — a special etiquette that gives us a sense of inclusion and belonging that is independent of our status in the everyday world. In this sense the pub is very much a social leveller — something that was apparent even in the Middle Ages. It's where people of disparate status and economic difference are mixed. A place that brings men, high born and low, into relation, fostering a propinquity that might secure, adjust or even threaten hierarchies.

Reasons to go to the pub

1. It's your birthday.

2. It's your friend's birthday.

3. It's someone you maybe met once's birthday, but you can't remember their name, so you mumble when it gets to that part of the song.

4. It's a Friday, and you've had a hard week at work.

5. It's a Saturday, the only day of the week when you're truly free.

6. It's a Sunday, and you need to drink to forget that you're back at work tomorrow.

7. Your football team won.

8. Your football team lost.

9. Drinking is the only way to make football tolerable.

10. George Osborne.

11. Because it's raining and the pub has a fire.

12. Because it's hot and the pub has a beer garden.

13. Because it's neither raining nor hot – perfect conditions for going to the pub!

14. You owe your friend a drink.

15. Your friend owes you a drink.

16. You have nothing else to do.

17. You have SO much to do that the pub is the only option.

18. It's Thursday, which is basically the new Friday.

19. How else are you meant to get through a Monday?!

20. Taylor Swift has just released a new album.

21. It's Christmas.

22. It's New Year.

23. It's Chinese New Year.

24. It's 5pm SOMEWHERE in the world.

25. It's Wednesday and it feels like the week will never end.

26. A glass of red is good for your health, don't you know.

27. You're supporting the local economy.

28. You're cripplingly lonely and it's the only way to meet people.

29. You're on a first date, and getting drunk is the only way to break the ice.

30. Because you're on any date, and it's the only way you can express your emotions.

31. Dark beer contains fibre, and you once saw an advert that said fibre keeps you regular.

32. The prospect of Ed Miliband.

33. The reality of David Cameron.

34. Because you're Nick Clegg.

35. You like going to the pub.

36. It's your half birthday.

37. It's your cat's birthday.

38. It's your friend's cat's half birthday.

39. You got a promotion. :)

40. You got fired. :(

41. There's nothing on TV.

42. There's nothing on TV and you've literally watched ALL of Netflix.

43. You got dumped.

44. You broke your hand and the cold beer soothes the pain.

45. The pub has Jenga.

46. You're still struggling to get over the Red Wedding.

47. Your housemate is a dick and you need to get out.

48. You can't face watching Octoknob on The X Factor.

49. You really fancy some pork scratchings but can't justify eating them without a beer.

50. There will be tables available at this time of day.

51. You read the word "pub" in a book today and now you can't stop thinking about it.

52. You dumped somebody.

53. You have a strict "three-drink minimum" rule before you can order a dirty takeaway, and you REALLY want a dirty takeaway.

54. Because you stalked your crush and know they're going to be in the pub.

55. Breaking Bad left a hole in your heart that can only be filled with alcohol.

56. You fancy the person who works behind the bar.

57. Because the pub offers a wide selection of real ales, and it would be rude not to try all of them.

58. Because it's on the way home from work.

59. You're hungover and require hair of the dog.

60. You have a crippling alcohol dependency.

61. You need to get off Twitter and try talking to people in the real world.

62. It will be a great place to send Snapchats from.

63. There is an excellent pub dog.

64. There is an excellent pub cat.

65. There is an excellent pub bearded dragon.

66. The voices in your head told you to.

67. Because no great story starts with "I was on my sofa watching Come Dine With Me".

68. It's showing the football.

69. It's showing the rugby.

70. It's showing the American football.

71. It's showing the snooker.

72. Because pubs always have tatty copies of John Grisham and Stephen King novels along the windowsills and you can't get enough of that shit.

73. Because you managed to get through the day without a drink and therefore you deserve a drink.

74. It's much nicer than your flat.

75. If anything you've got too much money and need to get rid of some of it.

76. You have a friend visiting.

77. You're alive, and if that's not worth celebrating, what is?!

78. It's winter.

79. Because drunk-texting your ex only ever ends well.

80. You don't have any glasses and home and you need to steal some.

81. It's National Going to the Pub Day.

82. The clocks have gone back. Or forward. You can't figure out which. Either way, beer.

83. It's the best way to paper over the cracks of your inevitably doomed relationship.

84. You never know, Taylor Swift might be in the pub.

85. You've run out of alcohol at home.

86. Because as if you have the energy to cook a roast yourself.

87. If you spend another second reading comments on the internet you'll lose all faith in humanity.

88. Someone asked you to.

89. You saw a spider in your house and so you live in the pub now.

90. Because, let's be honest, a Scotch egg and a pork pie is the dinner of champions.

91. Because sometimes you actually have to see a Wetherspoon's to believe it.

92. It has free Wi-Fi.

93. Pubs are an important part of our identity.

94. Everyone needs a local.

95. Even Taylor Swift.

96. Your friends are there.

97. You're going to pull a sickie tomorrow.

98. You're not going to pull a sickie, but being hungover at work makes it slightly more interesting.

99. Because beer tastes nice.

100. Wine, too.

101. Because it makes you happy.

102. Because why not.

103. Because you're British.

Welcome home, Sam!

Sam Gittins

The pub holds a firm place in British cultural history. It's a place that in many old towns and villages, is found both metaphorically as it is literally in the centre of it all. It is a place that is sometimes referred to as the heartbeat of the community. The pub can be a central focal point for a conversation and a meeting of mates and family and those you are trying to impress with a new designer jumper. It's where you'd take your girlfriend for a quick half, later to announce an engagement of marriage and in some cases to retreat from a divorce.

It is where you go to celebrate the birth or christening of a child, to raise a glass for those no longer with us and to settle a dispute over an argument started over who's got the hardest dad from your junior school days.

A place in British cultural history where you'll share embellished stories of a football away day and also a place to drown your sorrows of a cup game loss. The word can invoke as many tears as it can laughs. It's a place that the very chant of pub, pub, pub can be recognised as a call of local lads inciting a battle cry and one of lets go fucking mental.

The word pub could invoke a lot of meanings. The word pub can be suggestive as it can be literal. The word in itself can be a call for local lads for the start of a night out, as much it can be one of a simple, 'you up for the pub?, simply meaning let's go out for a few quiet ones. It's a place that can be a meeting spot for one of the more sensible ones in the family to pull you a side and 'ave a word in your shell like for the mischief you've gotten into.

It's the pub that invokes the memory of when I was en-route home to London from shooting a Netflix special in Warsaw, Poland. I should've been back home early evening, but as luck, or bad luck would have it, my flight got cancelled. It originally started off great. Couldn't of wished for a better way to see everyone off after grafting on set for the best part of a month. We are all in the airport bar having a good crack. Beer, laughs and all that goes along with banter at an airport bar, then I get the news I'm being left behind and not being able to get back to pastures greener for a good few hours. So here I am, stuck in Warsaw sitting at a bar with a bloke I've never met. Not a bad bloke, but not where I wanted to be and not where I needed to go.

So after a few good portions of the good stuff, I'm now boarding my plane, discovering that I will not be home until closing time of my local. You could say our lives revolve around the pub, and a comment I'm sure some have considered, but there's no way most would be able to squeeze everyone from their local in their living rooms. So, I've personally stuck with tradition and remaining loyal to my neighbourhood boozer. So after accepting my current situation, mixed with a little bit of frustration and the willingness to throw the cab driver a few extra quid, it's all engines go upon touchdown.

So here I am, only half hour to go before closing time and I'm walking through the doors of my local. Much later than I'd liked, but nonetheless I'm home. I enter the doors to be greeted by what I honestly thought was gonna be just a few pals. Instead, it must've been everyone local with an overwhelming avalanche of 'cheers!', and, 'welcome home, Sam!' After the insistence of the bar staff putting my suitcase in their trusted care. It was then I looked around, taking in everything that was waiting for me. It was here while clutching my pint glass and taking in the sights, the chatter of voices and the music in the background. It was then I knew what I'd missed. The pub, It's more than just your mates, more than those that support you. It's also banter, it's the neighbourhood characters, with the smiles and conversations that stood all around me. For me, that's the point, that's my story and that's a proper battle cruiser. Cheers!

Fish n Chips

It could be said there's nothing more British than fish and chips. The First fish and chip shop was opened by Joseph Mallen in 1860, London. Joseph's family were part of the local working-class community and to increase the family's income they started frying chips in the downstairs room of their house, to sell to locals and visitors. It was Joseph's idea to combine the chips (at that point and novelty in London) with fish he'd buy from a nearby fried fish shop, and it is from this date, the birth of the combination of the fish and chips tradition started.

The concept of a fish restaurant was introduced by Samuel Isaac, who owned a thriving wholesale and retail fish business in not just London, but stretching as far south as the south of England. Small in today's economy and business world, but in the years predating the breadth and strength of modern technology, a masterful achievement for the late 19th century.

It's been documented that Samuel Isaac's first restaurant opened in London, serving fish and chips, bread and butter, and a cup of tea for nine pence, and his popularity and success promoted an extension of the one single shop to develop into many more. Remembering a lot of stores and businesses of the time were trying to cater to more than the upper middle class, many small businesses were no more than small huts and make do stalls, so for the first fish and chip shop to employ carpeted floors, a sit down, table clothed service with waited staff, china and also with eating utensils made this a step up from the norm and an affordable attraction for the working class. Issacs stores could be found in as many locations stretching from London to the south coast of England.

Historical records show that in World War II, fish and chips were one of the few foods in the United Kingdom that were not subject to rationing.

The fish that is most asked and seen on all fish and chip shop menus is cod, but depending on geographical location and what may be favoured by the owner of the chippy, other variations can be found such as skate, haddock, plaice and occasionally salmon.

Traditional frying of the fish is going to be in a vegetable oil such as peanut oil, beef dripping or lard are commonly used. When it comes to the batter used on the fish, most places will use a simple water and flower batter. They will also use vinegar and baking soda to complete the process. There are some multi-generational family owned chip shops that may use a 'secret' but traditional method and ingredients for their batter on the fish.

Adding to your fish and chips is down to preference more than tradition. Most that frequent your local chippy in London and surrounding counties will tell you salt and vinegar is a must, ketchup for those that don't like the taste of malt vinegar but, in the south, never gravy.

Other add-ons or alternatives to fish will include saveloys, pasties, fish cakes, pickle onions, and mushy peas and various meat pies. No matter the time of year or political change, fish and chips continue to be a great London and of course British institution. A portion of kindness - The value of kindness found in a portion of tradition.

The Lifer

Performing an act for another human being, like cooking for them, is a form of altruism. This act can make people feel happy and connected to others. It was once written - Matthew 5:6 Blessed are they which do hunger and thirst after righteousness: for they shall be filled.

Prison can forcibly take all of the good things from you. But, to give something that will encourage a sense of trust, community, meaning, purpose, belonging, closeness, and intimacy, can be like that small ray of sunshine making its way through the small crack in the ceiling, a light under a closed door or the feeling of sunshine on your face through a small window in the wall.

They say courtesy and manners cost nothing. To some, providing for another, not looking for anything in return or any acknowledgment is a testament, that you are still human, have a soul and undoubtedly a place in the world.

I have a routine. It's not a routine I've chosen, or routine that I particularly enjoy, but it's one that I've stuck with for years now. When most people wake up in the morning, they lay awake for a while and then get up out of bed, pretty sure what events the day will bring. When I wake up, I lay with my eyes shut for a second or two, just hoping that my dream has ended and my life is not the way I remember. Once my eyes are open, I realize that my nightmare is real. My days consist of a tedious routine that is occasionally interrupted by a fight or an inmate complaining and telling a screw that, "it's a fucking liberty" or, "a piss take". Apart from that, the 12 hours of my day are pretty Mundane.

About 12 1/2 years ago I was at HMP Peterborough, I had been moved there, away from my co-defendants, for 'security reasons', - a term used with no accountability throughout the prison system. I was in an unusual situation, on remand for a murder that I had committed in self-defence, but with a firearm. The law had the opinion that I had gone to seek out an altercation with a drug dealer with the intent to kill him. This wasn't true. I was house on W-1, a remand wing, in a single cell. I worked on that servery, the hotplate area that inmates get their food from. I was number 1, the longest working member out four. Now, anyone that's been in prison will know that food holds a strange value on the wing. An extra piece of jam sponge can form friendships that last years. Alternatively, huge disturbances can take place around that servery over the smallest of arguments concerning ones cooked meal.

It was are you Saturday, I remember that because I had a visit that day and I always had visits on the Saturday. I was 'on the chips', serving them alongside slightly irregular rectangular shapes of breaded fish. There was also a choice of peas or corn. The queue was shuffling along quietly and at a regular speed. The occasional nod to a mate, a few, "yes, bruv" acknowledgements as the inmates moved by. About 3/4 of the way through, I spotted a new face. When you live with the same 120 people every day, I knew face is easy to see. He was late 50's I guess, he looked drawn and tired, his eyes were dark and hollow. He stood slightly hunched, looking very uncomfortable in his prison issue T-shirt and tracksuit bottoms. He was wearing black shoes, a sign that he had recently come from court. He looked scared. As he approached the hatch I watched him. I could see the nervousness making him tremble, he didn't look up, just sliding sideways with the sole purpose to get his food and get away from everyone around him as soon as possible. I guess he must've come in on the Friday court bus. Then he was in front of me, "chips, mate" I asked, he nodded. "What?" I said. I don't know why I did that, I'm guessing I just wanted to hear him speak, to acknowledge me. "Yes please" he said quietly, still not making eye contact. He shuffled off. I never eat food from the surgery. The most I'll ever take is some sweet corn to mix with my tuna, that I buy from the prison canteen. The food is tasteless, with little nutritional value, I'd rather not bother with it. But to some it's all they'll get, and as I mentioned before, it (food) can become a very important commodity. Once the servery was clean and all the lads were banged up, I walked back to my cell with a young screw to get locked up. I asked him about the fella I'd seen earlier and which cell he was in. He was in 1-16, ground floor, cell 16. I asked the screw for a favour, and we went to the cell and the screw opened the door. The inhabitant looked shocked that his door had suddenly swung open, and more dismayed when I handed him my fish and chips on a blue plastic plate. "Come see me later", I said as I pointed down the Landing. "Number 3". He nodded, but said nothing.

Jim, (not his real name) was on remand for mortgage fraud, about £750,000 if I remember rightly. He had been remanded as a 'flight risk' - someone who has the means to leave the country and avoid justice. His story was long and complicated; a tale of disabled children, a disloyal wife, gambling and debts. He told me it like he was reading from a book, not like it was the story of his life. I got the feeling he was somehow trying to disassociate himself from the chaotic life he had been living. I nicknamed him 'chips', which I think he found quite a comfort.

The lads on the wing accepted him quite quickly and also a few months he joined me on the server. It was a genuine bloke, no bravado like a lot of the idiots in the system, just a normal fella. He never really told me about his mental state when he first came into prison, the conversation never came up and, as he seemed quite a grounded man. I never questioned his stability. A few months later he went to court and got sentenced. He went guilty for all the charges, he was bang to rights anyway, so I don't think he had much choice. That evening, he came back to the wing and he was in a good mood. He seemed relieved that he now had a sentence and a release date. It's not unusual for people to act like that - sentences give a sort of closure, a date to aim for, and finish line.

Six weeks later he was transferred off to a D cat open prison; Brittania House in Norwich. He only ever wrote me one letter. I remember the letter started, "Guess who?, which I found a strange way to start. He then spent a few lines telling me about his new accommodation and the fellas that were in there. He told me his family had forgiven him and his kids had visited. He told me he was looking forward to the future and getting things back on track. But the last five lines of the letter had me in shock, feeling like I could hardly breathe, and a little dizzy. He wrote, "After I went back to myself that night I prayed for my family, I wrote them a suicide letter and I decided it was time to die. Your fish and chips saved my life. Thank you, forever your mate, chips x"

The British Seaside

Ever since the Victorians took a fancy to the coastal areas, that is commonly referred to as the Seaside, the social trend has never really stopped. The appeal of the British coast wasn't exclusive to any class or age and being an island race, the English have always best represented their social and cultural identity by promoting their love for the coastal traditions found on most of her shores.

As with so many things in modern times, the practice of 'going on holiday' is said to have originated with the Romans. This is largely believed to have been down to their success with their empire building and the fact they'd engineered a period of peace, traveling Roman citizens were able to explore their now newly gained lands in safety, but then came along the Dark Ages; not exactly a time for bagging up some sandwiches and a few bottles of the good stuff and heading to the coast, as the mere need for survival and preserving the family was seen president over a weekend jolly up. So, travel was limited to people occasionally traveling to neighbouring villages for religious festivals.

Later on, in Tudor times, only the rich and royals got to travel (this wasn't on the scale of what is done in today's terms of travel), from the safety and sanctuary of their prominence and lands, but more so to simply boast and celebrate with news (births of new princes and princesses) and raise their profile with their fellow aristocracy, their immediate social and economic brethren and of course the 'people'. This practice was called a "progress" and hundreds of people would join the procession. By the 18th century, the idea of taking a grand tour of Europe became standard for young social elites and privileged youth. They would visit France, Germany, Switzerland, Italy and more for a summer, before going home, committing to their families, in either industrious or upper middle-class dealings and of course getting married.

The Industrial Revolution gave birth to the steam train, so when bank holidays were introduced in law (1871) the working class could get away to the beach for a couple of days.

Holidays to Butlin's (holiday camps) became commonplace in the 1930s, and after World War II, when a two-week paid holiday was introduced, even more people began taking holidays. The affordability of the family car also saw a huge rise in the attraction of a weekend at the sea side.

The 1960's saw seaside trips begin to fall out of favour with British tourists, as rising wages increased the popularity of overseas package holidays, and being there's a truth to us brits being a sea fearing race, we'd welcome seeing lands showing more exciting and exoticness than a trip to Bognor, and as the numbers have shown how we holiday has evolved so much over time, but there truly isn't anything more quintessential than a trip down to the seaside. Plus, a few would further argue, why go from the simplicity of a day trip to seaside towns by train instead of spending up to half a year planning the worldwide trip of a lifetime and equal as much saving? But, there's now a hardious loyal part of the population that have shown in following years, the popularity and accessibility being a major factor, the great British seaside gained its place back in the 'best of British things to do'.

It's no secret, England and her surrounding neighbours aren't afforded the luxury of great weather year-round, as my grandfather once said, "Us brits don't shelter from the scornful weather, we embrace it". So, at the first sign of some half decent weather, the population en-masse would flock from the familiarity of their Monday to Friday routine, for a bit of fresh air and a day at the beach. That's not to say, England and her population, with all that she has to offer, has to resort to a few simple standard pleasures, as even with a level of self-bias and the leaning of a few hardened traditional routine rituals for many, there are many towns and places to visit when the sun decides to put her hat on. But, there's always been something special with the attraction of a sea-side town and how those places allow the great British public to feed their pining need for a coastal visit, drop their stiff upper-lip conservative values, and simply act a bit silly on a day out.

To see the vast horizon and feel the spacious and free environment that being on the seashore promotes, is something that can't be simply spoken about, only enjoyed first-hand. The fresh air, with the sound of the waves lashing against the pier promotes the traditionalist within us all. The bustling crowds consisting of 'down for the day' families, teens and early twenties on their first dates, football lads and stag do's and even the mods and rockers revival groups, reminiscing of their clashes on the beaches are traditions seen in most coastal towns. The landscape dotted sea fronts with small brightly painted beach huts (for the posh lot), penny arcades, small gift shops selling sticks of rock and penny sweets. Kiss me quick hats, postcards, that you'll probably never send, Donkey rides, Punch and Judy puppet shows, Fish and chips and burger bars. The British pub, cafes, ice cream vans, candy floss sellers and countless bed and breakfast overnight stays off the main streets, are all a testament to not only tradition, but also a time shared between generations. A few tea rooms are found within some coastal areas, but with the reinvention of corporate owned, chain branded froth filled coffee shops, they're unfortunately becoming less popular. A little further inland you'll also have caravan parks for the more frequent visitors. Some even come with a seasonal club house, with one hit local wonders performing ritual timeless classics with stand-up comedians, magic shows and for the beach hut owning city dwellers, you can occasionally find a cabaret show with a meal thrown in.

The English seaside beaches, typically aren't given their fair amount of credit. With horror stories shared worldwide, of rock and stone filled beaches, exaggerated tales of freezing cold waters and untruthful stories of unwelcoming locals, visitors aren't often drawn to a British beach. But, with a little bit of research and internet browsing, most will find some beaches are worth more than any critics review. There's nothing more fulfilling as a parent to see your children and in many cases grandchildren playing on a sun-lit, sand filled beach with their first bucket and spade, making attempts to build a castle big enough for the whole family and digging a whole deep enough to reach China. It is also the beach you'll find rock pools for the Charles Darwin's and biologists to explore and bring back creature filled shells and buckets of seaweed to give to many a parent, who's then forced to receive this unwanted gift.

From deck chairs to donkey rides, a brief history of what was once found within a trip to the sea side

Donkey rides

First documented in 1895 in Bradington. It's likely the donkeys were originally working animals for the cockle industries around the coastal area. Common fashion was the donkeys having their names on their nose burns. This would help sell a ride, as children would often pick a name they liked.

Fish and chips.

Even though having its origins firmly stapled within the working class of London, this working- class meal found its way down to popular spots that would then feed the hordes of hungry day trippers who wanted something that was both affordable and they were familiar with.

Seaside rock

Originally sold at Fairgrounds around the 19th century. An ex-miner named Ben Bullock from Burnley began manufacturing sticks of brightly coloured lettered candy at these home-based sweet factory in 1887. Bulluck sent his first batch of rock to retailers in sunny Blackpool and it was a success. The craftsman, who still make it by hand today are called sugar boilers.

Ice cream cones

Swiss immigrant Carlo Gatti made ice cream affordable when he first set up an ice cream stand outside Charing Cross station in 1851. He sold scoops in shells for a penny. History has shown, Gatti built an ice well to store ice that he'd cut from Regents Canal. When his business expanded he imported ice from Norway. Ice cream cones also become popular in the 19th century after they appeared in St. Louis during the world fair in 1904. A common story told is an ice cream seller ran out of cardboard dishes, but by chance in the next booth was a Syrian waffle maker who offered to make cones by rolling up his waffles. It's here the ice cream cone is said to be born.

The deck-chair

The use of a single broad strip of canvas, originally olive green in colour but later usually of brightly coloured stripes, has been credited to a British inventor named Atkins in the late 19th century, although there's been some dispute to the originality of the 'folding chair', who invented it in more modern times, and the idea itself actually going back to the Bronze Age.

The seaside pier

Piers were first built to accommodate upper-class travellers, allowing them to alight from steamers without getting their feet wet, but they soon became attractions in their own right. Now those same piers have been restored to their once former glory and splendour can be seen lightly lit and lined with small stalls, shops and arcades.

Punch & Judy

This legendary puppet show has its origins in the Commedia dell'arte street theatre of 16th Century Italy. The figure of Punch is derived from the Neapolitan stock character of Pulcinella, which was anglicized to Punchinello. The figure who later became Mr. Punch made his first recorded appearance in England on 9 May 1662, which is traditionally recognised as Punch's UK birthday. Punch and Judy began to emerge during the Restoration period which was around 1660, a period during which art and theatre thrived. The show is performed by a single puppeteer inside the booth, known since Victorian times as a professor or punchman, and assisted sometimes by a bottler, who stirs up the audience outside the booth, introduces the performance, and collects the money. The bottler might also play accompanying music or sound effects on a drum or guitar, and engage in back chat with the puppets, sometimes repeating lines that may have been difficult for the audience to understand. In Victorian times, the drum and pan pipes were the instruments of choice. Punch is a manifestation of the Lord of Misrule and trickster figures of deep-rooted myths. Punch's wife was originally called Joan.

BEACH BABIES

Martin Knight

In the early 1960s, not many people holidayed abroad. Not from where I came from, anyway. On our mantlepiece stood a miniature model Swiss chalet which had a key at the back which if you wound up would play a tune. It was a gift from our Auntie Margo who had somehow managed some European travel. This was a feather in the family cap; mantlepiece proof that someone in our extended family had been "abroad". Mum labelled it as an ornament. Today, if someone brought that back from a holiday and gifted it to you there would likely be a smile and a thank you and then you'd furtively lob it over your shoulder. (I would pay good money to have that music box now, actually).

We, as a family, were not in a financial position to holiday at all until the mid-1960s. Money was tight. Not too tight to mention. The lack of it was mentioned a lot in our council house. But, in about 1964 we finally managed to travel to the Isle of Sheppey to stay in Auntie Margo's caravan – Treetops. Hang on? Where did Auntie Margo get all this money from? A poor Battersea girl to boot. I must look into that. Treetops was on a caravan park at Warden Point and we adored our few snatched days there. Sheppey must have been one of the first coastal areas to be colonised by Londoners. South London cockneys, mainly, who would have enjoyed the annual hop-picking holidays in the Kent countryside as children and who now were buying or renting wheeled accommodation next to the seaside funded by a rising standard of living even for the common man.

A photograph survives of that holiday of me, my five siblings and Mum and Dad on a bench by a shop in Eastchurch. We are eating ice creams. Twenty or so years later I met my wife and discovered she was born in Eastchurch and lived her first seven years there. The shop we bought the lollies from belonged to her aunt. Valerie could have been inside sleeping in her pram for all I know. It's a small world. We loved Sheppey and when I went back half-a-century later I realised it wasn't a patch on other seaside towns from a holiday-maker's point of view. That's why the caravans were in the financial reach of the working classes. If Kent was the garden of England, Sheppey was the bit where you kept the metal dustbins.

The seaside was the pull. We were so excited to go and to be there but how did we know about the attractions of the seaside when we had never been? The next year my parents scraped the money together to holiday for a whole two weeks in Walmer, also in Kent. Our accommodation was to be an old railway carriage shorn of its wheels and sitting on concrete blocks on a scrap of wasteland next to Walmer Railway Station. On route we sat in a single train carriage as a very happy and excited family singing Ticket to Ride by the Beatles. Concrete and Clay by Unit Four Plus Two was also riding high and through those songs I can date that first long holiday as 1965. Above the window was a sign ordering DO NOT LEAN OUT OF THE WINDOW. I decided that just as soon as I could travel without adults I'd be leaning my head out of the window.

I think the package was bought direct from British Rail and came with free travel for all of us across the south coast railway network. The excitement of sleeping in a real Pullman railway carriage complete with emergency cord, buffet and British Rail livery was joyous. Especially, for Dad. Each day we went out from the carriage and visited Deal, Dover, Sandwich, Broadstairs and beyond. In the evenings us children went next door to the station where the stationmaster, who I remember was called Gerry, allowed us to collect tickets from smiling commuters. We were the railway children before The Railway Children. Those daily trips from the carriage were organised by Dad like an army expedition. He had an army back-pack he took everywhere, even to the shops, his army groundsheet he laid out on the beach or the grass and we all drank squash out of his army jerry can. When we got up from our beach picnic to walk back to the nearest railway station, he'd command us to 'Fall in' – only half joking. Although he served in the Royal Army Medical Corp you'd never have known as his language was peppered with nautical and oceanic references throughout his life. When a targeted destination came into view on our long, tiring walks, be it a castle or a bus stop, he'd declare 'Land Ahoy'. When he was rounding us kids up for tea, he'd call us landlubbers. Sometimes he'd rock from side to side, standing in the kitchen (or galley) as if effected by the movement of the waves. Threatened punishments for bad behaviour normally included walking the plank. Scurvy was a disease always lurking under the surface at our house.

After a couple of years at the railway carriage we could afford more space and a slightly more salubrious resort – Hastings. Dad had been taken there as a kid. For me, it became a magical place and even now fifty years later as I enter the town, I feel a frisson of glorious memories combined with lost sensations and smells from my childhood. Hastings was everything a seaside town should be. It was dominated by two hills - the East and West - both boasting funicular railways and nestled in between was the old town characterised by tiny fisherman's' cottages, pubs and quaint shops. It had a castle, a pier, a theatre, a boating lake, amusement arcades, shops selling rock, buckets and spades and ice cream galore. We had our own money, us kids. We saved our pocket money and paper round earnings for the holiday each year. This money was ours and we could spend it how we pleased. Laurence and I would head straight to the pier where we played the penny machines. It was not unheard of for me to spend (lose) all my brown pennies and halfpennies, three penny bits, sixpences, florins and even half-crowns in the first couple of days. Laurence lasted longer. Careful with his money he even held ambitions of making a profit, but the laws of the penny arcades eventually even applied to him.

The arcades were heaven and I could spend a day in one. Even now as I pass and hear the whizzing, jingling and jangling I experience that surge of excitement. There was a horseracing game Laurence and I played on where you backed jockeys in each race and if your jockey won you doubled or trebled your money. The names of the jockeys give away how old this old machine was even then: Harry Wragg, Gordon Richards, Charlie Smirke etc. If a jockey let me down, I'd choose another in the next race. Laurence would stick with one pilot and keep backing them until he won. He inevitably lost, but not as much as me. I would then gravitate to the What The Butler Saw machine. He didn't see much. A lady putting on stockings, perhaps. Then there was the grab machine where if you persisted you could win a furry animal that cost a fraction of the cost in the gift shop next door than the seven tries you had winning it. Rolling pennies down a slope and hoping they'd land in between two lines was good as well as the one that pushes the pennies over the edge. Every hour or so I'd fish into my pocket produce a half-crown and take it over to the surly man in the booth. I'd stand on tiptoe to hand it to him.

'Whadoyawannitin?' he'd grunt while looking over my head. 'Pennies, please.'

And the old brown pennies would come hurtling out a long shute into a bowl where I greedily scooped them into my pocket. Momentarily and entirely falsely I felt like a winner. It took me some years to understand why my Dad didn't want to change his silver into pennies when was so much more of it. We'd dawdle back me and Laurence. Pockets lighter. Stopping to throw pebbles into the sea. Laurence could skim and bounce a stone. Mine just plopped in. And as dusk fell, we'd have one last climb into Cat's Cave on the rocks on the West Hill before jumping over the wall into the garden of the big Victorian house and through the back door where undoubtedly Mum would be about to serve up a dinner. Glorious days.

It was at Hastings I first came face to face with Mods and Rockers. I watched them from a safe distance as they marauded up and down the promenade and the beach, fighting and surging using the very British stripy deckchair as missiles to assail one another with. The film Quadrophenia faithfully reprised those heady days of teenage rebellion although Brighton, not Hastings, was the scene of the action. Brighton was the more famous battleground and it was to Brighton that my seaside visiting turned as soon as I got wheels.

Brighton had a very different feel to it than Hastings. Public perception, certainly mine, had been influenced by Graham Greene's book Brighton Rock and moreso the classic noir film that followed. It was a town of small-time crooks, retired London gangsters, blousy prostitutes, surly youths and rowdy day trippers. When I got there at weekends in the mid-1970s it was 30 years after Brighton Rock, but I imagined Pinky was still there. Older, but still dangerous. Also it was an altogether more serious, more mature proposition. If they were brothers Brighton would be Noel and Hastings Liam. Several carloads of us would travel in noisy convoy the 50 miles south in Ford Anglias, Cortinas and Corsairs. We'd drink in the pubs before entering Sherry's, the nightclub on the front. Sometimes there would be fights but we soon learned not to underestimate the locals. Brighton had its own rough element who were very happy to take it to a bunch of pissed up Londoners, or in our case Surreyites. Sometimes I visit these wonderful places from my childhood and youth. Hastings hasn't changed. The charm remains. It is a town that waits patiently in the queue to be gentrified, modernised and homogenised. But when it finally does that scruffy, individualistic charm will be lost.

I went to the railway carriage just last summer. Small blocks of flats had been prised into the area around Walmer railway station, I could have sworn they were open fields when we went. The wasteland that the carriage stood on remained but no carriage. The footprint not much bigger than an envelope now. I felt the ghosts of who we were then and looked vainly on the ground for a remnant of our visits. The arm of a doll. The remains of a Dinky car. My Dad's tobacco tin. Alas, no such luck.

The Doner Kebab

One of the World's Most Popular Spitted Meats

When it comes to fast food, each country has its favourites. Each country and continent will have its traditions and cultural disciplines when it comes to food, but London walks all over any city when it comes to the cultural diversity in terms of foods. As much as there's opinions on what's the best, is largely down to simple preference. Of course, this same opinion is biased, but that's why they call it an opinion; but most will agree a persons biased opinion is exclusively reserved on their personal experience. Now, London, much like most English cities, are spoilt with its options on eating out, and not a single person can honestly say that from their time spent coming in from a night out; whether it be to or from a pub or a club, have they ever not indulged in the richness and beautiful experience of one of the finest cultural imports from the once great Ottoman Empire - of course, we're talking about the Turkish doner kebob.

To have and an appreciation of most things is to understand not only the background, but also the value it brings to a person's life, and in many a person's humble opinion, none equal to that of the pride and joy of having possession of one of these meat, sauce and vegetable pieces of art.

To learn the history of the spitted meat, you only have to google the very word, 'kebab'. Firstly, you'll be given some variations and spellings differences. The next and largely disputed by many is the claim that the kebab comes from another country! Even though the word kebab (which has never been disputed by anyone as the only name it's known by) which actually translates from the Turkish word meaning spitted meat, and is properly spelled with a 'P' due to Turkish phonetics date back to the days of the Ottoman Empire. Another slight and earlier change of the kebab was the actual cooking, or roasting of the meat. Ottoman chefs changed the process when roasting the animal by realising that when the meat was spitted horizontally, due to fat dripping down from the spitted meat into the fire below, this caused the flames to flare top and singe the meat. The Ottomans then turned the spit vertically kept the flames far enough away from the rotating meat and not affect the meat under their care.

According to quite a few reports, Germany is the current kebab capital of the world and, with an estimated 17,500 kebab slingers in the country, it's easy to see why Germany self-crowns its-self as the kebab capital of the world. Not to add petrol to an already fiery argument with any country, the fact a country has more kebab outlets, doesn't justify the claim it's the innovator of the spitted meat, as most will agree it's about quality over quantity. But, whatever the opinion, Germany certainly has given the ottoman sandwich a global platform.

According to Yavuz İskenderoğlu, his grandfather Iskender Efendi as a child in 1850's Bursa, had the idea of roasting the lamb at his father's restaurant vertically rather than horizontally; it was a success, and some years later became known as döner kebab. Around the late 1800's, the dish took its current ready-to-cut embodiment largely thanks to Iskender Efendi of Bursa. Bursa is the fourth-largest city in Turkey and the site of the Uludag mountains, which the Greeks originally referred to as Olympos - but should not be confused with the mythical Mount Olympus, even if you consider kebab to be the food fit for the gods. After World War II, mass migration and either Memhet Aygun in 1971 or Kadir Nurman in 1972, the kebab found a new home in Germany. It's worth mentioning that both Memhet Aygun and Kadir Nurman received glowing obituaries in British newspapers.

So now that we're all caught up, assuming some are over who invented and accepted the fact the kebab came from Turkey, we can safely say we're at present day England and the success of the Turkish kebab. The upside-down pyramid meat spins, where only the outer inch is actually cooked, leaving the inside layers frozen and uncontaminated. The kebab itself on the spit averages around 200lbs of meat, that is usually comprised of 95% veal, with a small chaser of lamb. During production, the meat is seasoned with spices like paprika and cumin, then soaked in a yogurt-based marinade to break down the cellular structure. The first doner kebab could be found in London any-where between the 1940's -1960's (as immigrants from Turkish, Cypriot and Kurdish communities arrived in search of a new life and as with all migrant populations, the people of these communities brought their customs and cultural influences with them, including the Doner Kebab). It wasn't until 1966 that the famous doner kebab – cooked on a vertical spit – first appeared with the opening of the Hodja Nasreddin Kebab House by Çetin Bukey and Kojay Hüseyin in North London's Newington Green.

Chicken kebabs came on the scene in the '90s, along with the popularity of other fast food options, kebabs had to take a healthy turn (no pun) and accommodate other types of meat eater. The German kebab industry has more kebab stands than McDonald's or Burger Kings combined, but with that level of competition, it's easy to understand why the kebab industry had to bend a little in terms of its traditional content.

By 2006, kebabs had become the 7th most popular takeaway food in the UK, but demand continued to grow and between 2014 and 2016, Kebabs made it to the 4th most popular takeaway food in the UK behind pizza/ Italian, Chinese and Indian food. Today, the Kebab Industry is reportedly worth £2.2 Billion to the British economy, employs thousands of people and has become an integral part of British Culture.

Most kebabs are eaten with lettuce, tomato, cabbage, onion, but there are plenty of regional variations, some places in the U.K also use a combination of a chili and or curry sauce. There are of course variations with the content, but this is largely due to the wants and interpretations of what a kebab should have also respective of the geographical location of the eatery and what is typically available (more than what should be preserved to merit the cultural identity of the kebab). A typical variation of the Turkish kebab is the actual change of name; Greeks call it gyro. Gyros tend to be more popular in the US, but despite the lack of major chains, most cities have a few small family run stores, as well as plenty of street vendors dishing out late-night kebabs. Another name for the kebab is the Shawarma.

The Stolen Kebab - a true story

Vinnie Stone

Probably one of the most memorable and personal experiences of a kebab in a ritual known as a night out with your mates. This was back in the 1980's; the local pub was common-place, there was a lot less politics in your life and your weekly routine was a much simpler one.

A few of us had decided, like most weeks, we would grab something to eat on our walk home from the pub. It typically narrowed down to one of a few choices. Pizza, a chicken burger of sorts or a kebab. For me, the kebab would always win hands down out of those three. So, here we are, shuffling into the local kebab shop, and much like each week, we find ourselves trying to scrape enough together for a last desperate meal with what you had in your pocket. But, like most weeks after the pub, you were not left with much. The low funds wasn't down to a lack of thought or planning ahead, the 'meal after' simply wasn't as important at the time as getting in the rounds and trying to get lucky with a local sort. Here we would all agree, we wasn't asking for much from life, simply enough for than now very important last meal before bed.

Another typical situation, would be trying to get a quid or two out of one of your mates, as the now flash-backs of that extra round and a few shots, was at the time a good decision, but mistakes are made and the regret is soon forgotten with the low mutterings and sounds of, "Ah, good I've got enough!, "Yeah, made it, me too!" From within the group. Like the discovering of a new continent by an ancient explorer or a scientist who's finally cracked it after finding a cure for a life threatening disease, you're happy as a pig in shit when you finally add up what change you have in your pockets to get not only a kebab, but also chips and a can of coke; fucking bonus! Now, like most groups of mates in any city or county, there was always one that never had any money, no matter the weather.

For the purpose of this story, I will simply refer to our penniless mate as soap. He was a slippery little fucker that would get out of paying for anything, but being a childhood mate, we tolerated his 'broke routine' week in, week out, as deep down he was a good person and more often than not the brunt of our jokes.

So here we all are, scraping together what we had, also trying to get enough money together for the now begging for mercy soap to also have a kebab.

So we're ready for the what would feel like a 10 mile journey, but in reality a 20 minute slow-staggering shuffle, and start to plan our walk home. With kebabs, chips in hand and cans of coke hanging out of our jeans and jackets pockets, we leave the sanctuary and tendering smell of the brightly lit kebab shop and head out into the cold and early dark hours of Sunday morning. No sooner had we exited the kebab shop doorway and all started to eat our kebabs, when soap dropped something from his pocket, it was his bank card. With absolutely no defence or excuse, along with some added influence of half a dozen largered-up teens on his case, soap agreed it was time for him to pay back a few quid he had out of us that night and many nights before. Luckily enough for us, we were walking past a cash point machine.

With a group effort and a few point men giving guidance and direction to soap, we get to the bank and all eyes are on soap to start the process. We've all huddled around soap as he puts his cash point card into the machine. Some within the group may have defended our huddling action as a means of staying warm and getting some support, as here you have to appreciate and take into consideration we were a group of lads who are fresh from the local, not exactly at our best and also leaning sideways. Some may go as far to suggest we were offering a level of safety and security in a dangerous and cruel world, but me, I was in need of some much needed returned funds, as next Friday's pay packet was an eternity away.

So what would be on any other day, a simple process of putting your card in the wall and getting out your hard earned cash being an easy one, turned south very quickly. Now, this was a time when certain Cash-Point machines would have a protective piece of plastic covering the keypad. The keypad would only become exposed after you put your card into the machine, resulting in the plastic cover slowly sliding back exposing the keypad allowing you to then push the buttons.

So here it goes, as soap reluctantly puts his card into the slot, we all watch the protective cover reveal the keypad, we all start to lean in closer as if the holy grail itself has now been exposed. In fairness and in his defence, most people would've done exactly the same as soap, putting the kebab down so as to master the delicate process of pushing four numbers whilst under the influence of a scrupulous amount of alcohol.

Much to soap's frustration, he could not remember his pin number. After some deliberation and what was on par with enough huffing and puffing to convince any passer-by that someone within our group was in need of some oxygen, soap couldn't remember 4 simple numbers. Now as some of you may remember, back then, and as a means to prevent theft and fraud, after what must have been 3 or 4 attempts of failed number pushing, the bank put in safety measures to retain the card and close access to the keypad. What happened next couldn't have been scripted by even the likes of John Sullivan or Harry Enfield.

Soap couldn't remember his PIN number, this resulted in the plastic screen coming down covering the buttons. To his horror, soap now realised his kebab was left in the same place he had put it down - on the keypad that was soon to be covered by the slow moving plastic covering. In a fruitless effort, soap, and after the biggest shriek and gasp-less panting, managed to get just the pitta bread part back as the plastic cover came down back into its original place, leaving behind a visible, still steaming, hot pile of lamb meat and the vegetables that were once inside the pita bread he was now holding in his hands. The look of horror and anguish on his face promoted a group of London lads to be in absolute tears of laughter. What didn't help was none of us were even close to eating half way through our kebabs, and no matter how much protest and begging, no one was parting with any of their kebab. Of course, soap was not happy and under protest, walked off sulking and calling us names in his departure in the opposite direction. Now, some would suggest this was pure karma served best for all parties involved - none of us with any chance of monies being returned from soap, and soap was now one cash point card less, no chance of getting any money from his account until the next bank day opening and also not having the company of either a kebab or his mates that cold early Sunday morning.

The following week, and as predictable as the days and months in the calendar, the same lads, the same routine of not pulling a bird or getting a result, meant the same group agreeing after the pub, the best option was a kebab. But this time, soap, insisted he would wait outside the kebab shop. Even after the offer of me buying him a kebab, he said he wasn't hungry and would wait down the road. Upon my delayed entering into the kebab shop, I'd walked in on half a conversation, only to hear soap had recently been banned from the kebab shop. Being locals, we always got along with most staff, whether it be the local pizza place, kebab shop or Chinese Takeaway, we'd often be treated to the stories and hear about the misfits and trouble makers the staff had to put up with on a weekly basis, but to my astonishment, one of our own was now the making of an embarrassing story. "How the fuck can anyone be banned from a kebab shop?", I asked. We learned from the owner of the shop that soap had gone back the previous week from his kebab disaster, placing his now empty pita bread on the counter and insisting they had forgotten to put in the meat and vegetables that he had paid for from his earlier visit. Even after the owner played back the CCTV, several witnesses' favourable input, and the staff pointing out it was impossible for anybody not to notice there was no filling inside the pita bread, soap simply wasn't having it, resulting in him throwing a tantrum, kicking chairs and upsetting the counter staff. We apologized for his childish behaviour, meeting up with soap down the road, we tore the absolute arse out of him.

To this day whenever I speak with soap, I always remind him of that night. To date, I've never heard a story that would equal and merit that night of soap and his kebab stolen by the cash point machine.

The Sunday Roast

A shared belief is one of the most important meals of the week is the Sunday Roast. A time of the week when,

Typically, the modern family would gather for a hearty, over-indulging meal, that consists of a large gathering of direct kin and family for a celebration of what had been accomplished from a week's hard work and labour.

The name is a big give away, being the Sunday roast is served on a Sunday, but what isn't known is why this would be considered and respected more than any other meal of the week. It's been said by many an English patron, maker and practitioner of the Sunday roast, that it is the pinnacle and most iconic of English meals and a dedication of British cuisine.

One such article written in the history of English foods, claimed the French called the English of that era the 'rosbifs'; translated as the roast beefs.

This is largely due to beef being a favoured meat served with the meal and within the English diet.

Written and historical documents has also shown, The Sunday roast came to prominence during the reign of king Henry the 7th in 1485; the yeoman of the guard - the royal bodyguard- have been affectionately known as the beefeater, since the 15th century because of the reported account of their love and regular eating of roast beef.

History gives many references to the meaning, justification and historical start of the Sunday roast. The most read are based on two (of many) historical points on the origins of the modern Sunday roast. In the late 1700's during the industrial revolution in the United Kingdom, The Sunday roast originated in England as a meal to be eaten after church on Sunday. Being a common practice for all god-fearing English people, Sunday church was common place, so Eating a large meal following church services was a basic practice. The Sunday roast is common to all of the continent of Europe as with other Christian countries, but the Sunday roast variant of this meal is uniquely English.

The routine would have been to put an entire animal on a spit in front of the fireplace and spit roast the meat slowly. Obviously, large fireplaces weren't common-place within working class communities and households, but the same working class would instead drop off a more modest cut of meat to their local baker en-route to the church. The bakers would then use their empty bread ovens to cook and hand back to the villagers in time for lunch. Being that we've since moved on from large fireplace cooking, the modern oven now bakes the meat and other items going with the meal, but we still cling to the term Sunday roast.

The second opinion holds that the Sunday roast dates back to medieval times, when the village serfs served the squire for six days a week. Then, on the Sunday, after the morning church service, serfs would assemble in a field and practice their battle techniques and were rewarded with a feast of oxen roasted on a spit. The Sunday roast, being a favoured type meal, isn't reserved for just Sundays. Shortened to a roast, being served any day of the week, it's common place to find on any given day of the week, meat, baked or mashed potatoes, Yorkshire puddings, peas, carrots, cauliflower, parsnips, Brussels sprouts, runner beans, broccoli, and of course mint sauce and gravy, being served within the British house hold. It's worth mentioning that Christmas would also promote the roast, typically giving way to additional 'add ons' in terms of what would be included food wise.

The Sunday roast has also been a common meal served within a lot of pubs and restaurants. It has been said by some notable and traditionalists within certain English preservation clubs, The style and quality of the roast can also be a testament to the standard of authenticity of a traditional English pub.

With the Sunday roast being within the blood and making of all English folk, a famous patriotic ballad was once written on the very subject -

When mighty roast beef was the Englishman's food,
it ennobled our brains and enriched our blood.
Our soldiers were brave, and our courtiers were good
Oh! The roast beef of old England,
and old English roast beef!

The ingredients

Meat

Typical meats used for a Sunday roast are chicken, lamb, pork, or roast beef, although seasonally duck, goose, gammon, turkey and depending on your social circle and the time of year, game birds could be on the table.

Vegetables

Sunday roasts can be served with a range of boiled, steamed or roasted vegetables. The vegetables served vary seasonally and regionally, but will usually include roast potatoes - roasted in meat dripping or vegetable oil or gravy made from juices released by the roasting meat, sometimes the gravy could be supplemented by one or more stock cubes, gravy browning or thickening.

The potatoes can be cooked around the meat itself, absorbing the juices and fat directly (as in a traditional Cornish under-roast). However, many cooks prefer to cook the potatoes and the Yorkshire pudding in a hotter oven than that used for the joint and so remove the meat beforehand to rest and "settle" in a warm place.

Accompaniments - Common traditional accompaniments include:

Beef - Yorkshire pudding, suet pudding, English mustard or horseradish sauce.

Pork - crackling and sage - and - onion stuffing, apple sauce our English mustard

Lamb - mint sauce or jelly or red carrot jelly

The Family and the Sunday Roast

Scott Peden

The Sunday roast as it is affectionately known, is a quintessential British meal. However, it's one where the mere mention of it, fills me with feelings of nostalgia and romantic notions of days gone by.

I recall being a hyperactive child sitting around the dining table with my Mother, Brother and Sister, awaiting the appearance of Father from the kitchen to dish out the proverbial roast that he was concocting in the kitchen. He is an altogether amazing cook and is very militant when it comes to his cooking etiquette. Not a soul was allowed into the kitchen whilst he was cooking. It was his domain and we collectively knew that it was worth adhering to his rules, as the outcome was a culinary delight!

I distinctly recall the conversations of everyone's woes, joy and experiences of the week gone by and the expectation of the one about to begin. This was aptly combined with an abundance of anecdotes, stories and as always Glaswegian quick wit and humour from my Father, known as "The Patter".

I also recall being reprimanded for being too loud, or eating too fast, or teased by my older brother, but I also fondly recall being loved, accepted and surrounded by my family and the food was at the epicentre of this experience.

At such a young age, I didn't really think about the love and family unity aspect in the aforementioned situation, or neither the importance of it. However, now as a grown man, who has rocked and rolled with the ups and downs of life, I realise that family is the most important thing in the world and I am lucky to still have that family unit around me today and the old boy still knocks up some great food!!

We live such fast-paced lives where technology is advancing at an alarming rate. Social media ensures we have instant connections to the other side of the world at the touch of a button or screen, but we have become so lost and deficient in other aspects. How many of us sit down and talk? How many of us say how we really feel without fear of ridicule or judgement? That usually occurs when we are in the company and comfort of our loved ones and again, as previously mentioned, in the epi-centre of this is the food. So that's what the Sunday Roast means to me. Not so much the food even, but the people who to whom you share it with.

It means talking and spending time with those you love and being the true and authentic version of yourself. The version that only your family and close and trusted friends know. The one where your insecurities, fears, doubts, flaws, failures and triumphs are all on show in glorious techni-colour and the mask to the world is removed, yet you are still loved and accepted. I can honestly say there is nothing better than sitting with a stomach full of good food, surrounded by the love and warmth of your family, so please cherish it, because as time goes by, the table settings become less and less......

Now that is serious food for thought, pardon the pun...

Football

Football is a team sport that is played within most populated areas in the U.K. and the world. A team sport that is played with a single ball, or depending on the venue and personal budget, can be anything that'll tolerate being kicked up and down a street or around a school playground. A sport when played on a commercial level is a sport played between two teams of eleven players, but when played locally, comprises of how ever many people that are at hand and willing to play. It's a game that is played by 250 million players in over 200 countries, making it arguably the world's most popular sport. The game is played on a rectangular field called a pitch with a goal at each end. Local kids will employ an unscripted, but well-known set of rules - the unevened set of teams playing within a random area, with make-shift goal posts, using anything and no more than a 'will do' object, that'll be happily accepted as a substitute ball. Whatever your political beliefs or favourite page 3 girl is, the only objective is to put the ball between the two opposing posts and score a goal. Not forgetting your aging adults within any working-class community, (who still fancy their chances of being randomly picked from a magic hat and thrust onto the international platform of professional football) will also play in any given environment that physics and some laws permit. A common action by your aging adult English male leaving a local on a Sunday afternoon, with the opportunity and chance of passing any level ground, and if the sight and chance of a kickable object is within reach, don't be surprised to see an unruly, less than well balanced male give his best rendition of a life-saving goal scoring performance for the World Cup of his chosen year.

The most common and admitted story of football and its ancestral roots, tells that the game was developed in England in the 12th century. It was during this time, that the game closely linked with the sport that is identified with what is now known as modern day football, was played on evened grounds and areas; open fields etc. Early writings of the game suggest in addition to kicking the ball, players were permitted to punch the ball with their fists. This early form of football was also much more violent than the modern way of playing, causing considerable damage to the towns it was played in and sometimes lead to death. This lead to proclamations against the game, eventually forbidding the game to be played. But football type games would appear again in the streets of London in the 17th century. It would be forbidden again in 1835, but at this stage the game had been established in public schools.

It would be some time until what we would identify as modern football to take hold, as there was no clear distinction between what is known as rugby and football. Some favourable writings strongly lean towards the two sports being identified as coming into their own down to geography and some scholarly input.

The game was often played in schools and two of the predominant schools at the time were Rugby and Eton. At Rugby, the rules included the possibility to pick up the ball with both hands. At Eton, on the other hand, (no pun) the ball was played only with the feet and this game can be seen as a close precursor to modern football. The game in Rugby was called 'the running game'. while the game in Eton was called, 'the dribbling game'. Some have suggested the 'dribbling game' was more skilful and attracted a better class of English gentleman.

With an attempt to establish rules for the game two dates come up in most readings and writings on the history of the game. It has been recorded the first attempt to employ some standards and rules was at a meeting in Cambridge in 1848, but no final solution was achieved. Another important event in the history of football came about in 1863 in London, when the first Football association was formed in England. It was here the decision was made that carrying the ball with your hands wasn't allowed. Also decided at this historic event was the standardisation of the size and weight of the ball being played. Another consequence of the London meeting was that the game was divided into two codes - association football and rugby.

Over a period of time, further additions and changes would take place regarding the rules. The development of the game would also see some flexibility concerning what 'lines' could be crossed. The size of the team and club colours/ uniforms had also not been set. One surprising aspect of the game was the wearing of caps by the early players.

The sport was at first an entertainment for the British working class. Unprecedented amounts of fans, some would suggest up to 30,000, would see big matches in the late 19th century. Also, with the success and dominant placing of British subjects due to the colonisation and reach of the once great British Royal navy, the expansion of football reached to at least one third of the globe, securing an early success of football as the world's most popular game.

Football clubs have existed at earliest since the 15th century. But, without accurate sharing of information, the forming of local clubs, it is hard to decide which was the first football club. Some historians suggest that it was the Football Club formed in Edinburgh in the early 1800's. One common and accepted belief is the forming and noted clubs within school by the students. One such club was formed in Sheffield in the mid 1800's. Although, the oldest among professional football clubs is Notts County that is documented to have been formed in 1862.

But, none could argue an important step for the development of football teams was the industrialisation of 'modern Britain', allowing groups of people to socialise and meet in places such as pubs and churches. Football teams were established in the larger cities and with the new means of transport encouraged a population to move between cities and the country.

A Football Story - a fan and a supporter's promise

Author - TR

What is the game of football? It's more than just a game that we played as children. It's a game played by people in most places in the world; the beach, in a field and in the street. It is a game that is played by those who speak different languages, different cultures and who hold different beliefs. It's a game that is played for those that love or care for something more than themselves. Those who see more than a round object kicked up-and-down any length of service and that of what we call a football pitch. It's a game where the rules will differ only based upon the environment and the affair. A game between friends in the city streets, on the local field or a spare patch of ground that is now deemed your own. Two sides with one common belief - you have to win. It is a game that is shared and believed in by more people supporting any one sport and more than any other game played in the world. This is more than just football. It's a game shared between father and son, between brothers, between neighbours and between the kid down the street. It is a game of more than chance, it is something that you carry from the first day you're introduced to the game until the last breath you take on this earth. It is the early morning, the midday and the last game of the day. That tattered ball and that simple belief that you had as a child, you'll be their next striker for your chosen team; the holy Grail of a boys dream. You're not tested of your abilities or the colour of your face, only the belief and love of the greatest sport ever played. The beloved game of football - it is the day before, the morning of and the journey to. It's the meeting of friends, the love for your team and the belief in the players. It's the huddling together, all eyes forward and the hope and prayers of that one weighted word that justifies that social gathering. The heart wrenching, soul defying word that can warm the soul, fill your heart and ease most pain - goal!

It is also a game of both tears and sorrow, frustration and anguish, but it's a game that carries you home. The weekly talk, the seasons commitment and the honour of having a team you call your own. It's your coloured kit, the club's emblem and your favourite player. This is no longer just football. It is who you are, it is what you believe and what you are fighting for. It's a reminder of the player who once lived down the road, in the next city and then another country. But a player each of us can find in us all. It's a game that you carry with you through rain, through storms both sunshine and hail. A game that holds you high even on a cloudy day. It's always been more than just football.

The Good Things In Life

Irvine Welsh

Sometimes you don't choose the good things in life; sometimes they choose you.

When I first came to London as a seventeen-year old, after prolonged summer visits to relatives in the capital, despite some evidence, I had no idea that I would become a fan of West Ham United. In fact, the claret of the strip bore a strong resemblance to the maroon of Hearts, the much-loathed rivals of my boyhood favourites, the wonderful Hibernian FC. But the devil is in the details: to the discerning eye there is a big difference between the colour of a fine full-bodied wine, and a bloodied turd.

But even then there were a few daft wee hints that West Ham would become my club in my second home south of the border. I was still a contrary bastard as a kid, so I decided to wind up my fellow Jocks by declaring a liking for Bobby Moore. As England's World Cup winning captain, Bobby was utterly detested by my childhood peers. The playground punches and the scorn only strengthened my mulish resolve.

Also, more inexplicably, I had a Shoot picture of Johnny Ayers on my childhood bedroom wall. He was a ginger-headed squad player! This was like the wall of some kid in East London being adorned with a picture of Hibernian's John Hazel. Football does lead us into strange places.

It also takes us out of them. I used to spend a lot of the summer holidays at my aunt and uncle's place in West London. The local kids in Southall tended to follow either Chelsea or QPR. I always fancied that I would be a floating football fan if I ever moved to London, rather than rooting for one team. I was and will always be, obsessed with my local club, Hibernian, domiciled between Scotland's old capital, Edinburgh, and Europe's premier port Leith, where I hail from.

But I was drawn to London at an early age by those summer visits, and part of the attraction was football: all those teams! My Uncle Alec worked on the railways and in the sixties moved south with his job. There he met my Aunt Jessie who was a nurse in St Thomas hospital. Despite being on the other sides of the political spectrum, him a Scottish trade unionist and socialist, her a working-class Tory whose family worked in the Upstairs-Downstairs/Downton Abbey world of domestic service, they fell head over heels in love. They married and moved into a house in Fulham (when it was solidly working-class territory) and had two children, Alec Junior and Elizabeth. Due to the proximity of Chelsea football club, my Hearts-supporting Uncle became a fan. I got into going south on summer holidays, first with my parents, then, as I got older, on my own. By this time Alec, Jessie and family had moved to Somerset Road in Southall, which was the last white enclave in an area changed by mass Asian immigration.

Coming from a council scheme of 70's system-built flats, even a modest semi with a back garden seemed like a stately home. When I was 14 and bursting with hormones, there were two beautiful Asian girls living next door. They would sit in the garden, brushing each other's long, sleek raven hair, giggling when I came out to sit on the doorstep and catch some rays, and the odd glimpse of them through the threadbare bushes. The older one I fancied beyond sanity. Her name was Nootan, (that was how it was pronounced, I'm not sure of the spelling) and she was a total doll. We got to the stage of slipping notes to each other, but any further cultural cross-pollination was actively discouraged by the grown-ups, on both sides on the fence. One sweet kiss would have given me the keys to the universe, but absolutely no happy ending in this story. Certainly not for my poor Aunt Jessie who had to bung those surfboard-like sheets into the washing machine.

Anyway, back to that great antidote for sex, none other than king football. As a kid I was taken regularly to Stamford Bridge, which was a massive treat for me. Chelsea had become an iconic side due to their epic victory in the 1971 FA Cup final over 'dirty' Leeds, in what I think was the first live televised English cup final in Scotland. It was the team of Charlie Cook, Peter Osgood, Eddie McCreadie and Chopper Harris. The shed was like a smaller version of the Copland Road end at Ibrox. So it was set up for Chelsea to be my team in London, but the contrarian in me again kicked in. I decided I would support

West Ham. Well, Uncle Alec was a Jambo (Hearts fan) so I couldn't support the same team. Nope, I'd support the London team from the eastern part of the city, the dock area of the town. My first game at Upton Park was around 15, versus Everton. I set out across London on my own, taking the 207 bus to Shepherds Bush and a long tube ride east to Upton Park. The game was a cracker, a thrilling 2-2 draw. But it I was grabbed by much more than that: I felt immediately at home like I hadn't done anywhere else in London. I don't know if there's something about working class dock communities (and although Newham, like Southall, was changing ethnically, most of the support still came from those traditional East London communities or those displaced down the estuary) but I instantly felt incredibly comfortable in Upton Park. The aspiration to play passing, attacking football, to give talented local youths an opportunity to play for the club, and the biting wit of the fans, as likely to be deployed against home as opposition players, as well as their desire to make the match day experience for visiting supporters as 'memorable' as possible, was common to the culture of both clubs. I loved everything about the day, the bus and tube ride, the ground, the atmosphere, and the banter in the chicken run. (Even when I was on the receiving end of it: my Aunt Jessie had given me a rolled up plastic Mac, which a bunch of herberts ripped the piss out of me for. "Not outrageously fashionable. But practical. Sensible." One guy, (who would have only been a couple of years older than me) commented to his mates. They scrutinized me for the whole game, probably praying for rain, waiting me to put the ridiculous mac on over my Adidas cap-sleeved top and Levis, so they could really go to town.) Yes, it was a proper home from home. I'd found a place in London that I identified with and would continually be to down the years.

When I moved permanently to stay at my aunts, (utterly spoiled to fuck by her, while pretending to my mates back home I was living in a squat –it was the punk era) I kept up the pretence of being a generic London football fan, and would attend games at all the grounds.

Sometimes you don't choose the good things in life; sometimes they choose you.

At the Vortex in Soho, watching Gene October strut his stuff, I met this cool girl called Amy, and romance was in the air. She was right into music, and not just punk. She loved disco too, which you weren't meant to do, but we started going to all different gigs and clubs together. Amy was from Ilford and hated football. But her brother, Steve, was a West Ham fanatic. He and his mates adopted me and took me to games. Amy and myself split up, maybe partly because of this, as football won over romance and music. A couple of years later I heard Steve say to another mate who was asking how Amy was doing: "she's seeing some Tottenham cunt, when she could have been still going out with Irv." I knew I'd been fully accepted at that point. My best mate from that crowd was Ivsey, a practical joker who delighted in winding up everyone, friend or foe.

I got to know that journey well, the 207 bus from Southall to Ealing Broadway, and that great District Line trek out to Upton Park, where you knew you'd hit East London when the train started filling up with reassuring claret and blue. I made a couple of good mates in Southall, particularly Trevor Bryden, who

I'm still pals with to this day, and we'd banter about football, and West Ham and Chelsea. Trevor shared my contrary nature, and as a Chelsea fan, started supporting Hearts to wind me up.

Southall was often a tense place. We used to do some teenage drinking at the Hamborough Tavern on Uxbridge Road, where there was a major riot after the 4 Skins played there, and National Front supporters clashed with Anti-Nazi league protesters. I got into Madness and 2 Tone, and recall going to the Dublin Castle in Camden Town to see them play. As Suggs was a big Chelsea face, Trevor was a fan of the band and dragged me along. I'm so glad he did, the atmosphere generated by the band and their followers at those gigs was immense.

I got involved with a girl called Angeline, who was gorgeous and of mixed race. Her mum was from Trinidad. She was very political and got me into Workers Against Racism. A girl who had committed politics fascinated me, probably because my mum was a communist and trade unionist. WAR was associated with one of the far-left groupings that I never had a great deal of time for, but I was smitten with Angeline, so needs must. It was back when the first generation of Asian immigrants were very passive and therefore got excrement put through their letterbox's. (Their offspring would literally not take that shit.) WAR would send people round to sit there with baseball bats, as a deterrent. Now, from the benefit of age and experience, it's easy to say that most of the NF racists were cowards, and simply would go onto to easier pickings to spread their terror. But when you are the same age as them and with a bunch of largely poncey middle-class students who literally could not fight sleep, the perspective you have is very different. I would be shitting it holding a bat thinking 'what fucking good am I going to be if half a dozen skinheads come through the door?' But ultimately, the thought of getting into Angeline's knickers was much stronger than the fear. She was such a honey.

I would sit there with Angeline, nervous Asian couples and their scared kids, waiting on something to happen. It never did. I don't think I've ever known such tension; physical, cultural and sexual incubating in one room. I would walk out of there a paranoid wreck. That things never kicked off, I realized, was due to the West Ham connection. A mate, Les, who was involved with the NF in Hoxton, told me that he had said to the other fascists that I was okay and had to be left alone. Les was a sound guy; he'd just taken a wrong turning in his politics, and doesn't hold those views any more. I came from a monoethnic culture back in the Edinburgh schemes, where everyone was working-class and almost everyone was white. I saw my Aunt's reaction when her neighbourhood in Southall was transformed, and while opposing fascism and racism, had tried not to be too judgmental about people whose experiences had led them to holding views different to mine.

Football lads are often lazily seen as right-wing by the media, but I also saw West Ham lads involved in the News International dispute at Wapping. I actually liked that right-across-the-spectrum vibe: it made things interesting. Because of the proximity to the media there is always a highly performative element to London culture, which doesn't exist to the same extent elsewhere in the UK; that sense that you were auditioning for TV or the papers. It led to a type of grandstanding for easy notoriety, and a lot of young lads would act out in this way, (not all of them) while only holding racist views on a transitional, superficial level.

London was a great place to meet girls. In Edinburgh, you went out with a local bird and were in that working-class network- it like your life was all mapped out. But in London during punk, there were girls from all over and they had different horizons to the husband-house-car-baby lassies from the scheme back home. Obviously in local London neighbourhoods there was a lot of that mentality too, and many of my football mates at West Ham operated in the same way as my Hibs and Hearts buddies back home did.

West Ham and Hibs also had dedicated hooligan mobs. For all the notoriety and hysteria, these things were just a good day out, and you didn't need to be some frontline top boy to get involved. There was plenty of space back then in the seventies 'end taking' era for the gesticulating, occasionally windmilling clown, just there for the buzz, laughter and camaraderie. Though demonized beyond belief, the mobs were great institutions, which probably stopped a lot of youth from wasting away on booze and drugs. One of the most enjoyable bits of hooliganism I witnessed was from the Park Lane stand where the away support where cheering on this West Ham boy who was literally clearing the Shelf single-handed. It was quite a performance by big Cass Pennant who would later become a good mate.

I still had the conceit that I was something of a generic London football fan, than a dyed in the wool West Ham fan. I think it's because I wasn't a proper East End/Essex/London boy. I had therefore never grown up to detest Tottenham and Millwall, and through work and music, I had mates who followed all the London clubs.

I've mainly supported West Ham at home and in London derbies, but over the years have gone from Southampton to Newcastle to see them. Sadly, I've yet to see them play in Europe, an ambition I still cling to. I've done daft stuff too, for example in my early twenties I got arrested at Norwich and spent the night in the cells. There were two big farmers boys looking me up and down and I thought: this is going to be uncomfortable. Then I was grinning from ear to ear when some tasty West Ham lads were brought in. But they didn't know me from Adam and I was just a fucking Jock to them. I had to drop quite a few names to pull that one off!

Sometimes you don't choose the good things in life; sometimes they choose you.

I moved into a flat in Queensbridge Road in Hackney with my mate Stu, who was the most intelligent man I've ever met. Obviously he loved West Ham, and regarded Hackney as more East London than North London, and took an exception to the multitude of Gooners in the area. He was the loveliest guy in the world sober, but after a drink literally could start a fight in an empty room. Sometimes we made big plans to go to the Boleyn but never escaped the local pubs. My fault as much as his, it was dark time for me and we were a combustible duo. Through Stu, I became friends with Deb from Dagenham. A West Ham fanatic, she's like a sister to me, and she got me into buying a season ticket. "You're farking West Ehhhmm sahn!" She commanded. I obeyed.

Through music as much as football, I became friends with Paul Mulreaney and Grant Fleming. Paul is exiled in Australia now, but still one of my dearest friends. He hasn't really got to grips with this time difference thing, but following a win over Tottenham, Arsenal or Chelsea, I'll get treated to the most eccentric version of I'm Forever Blowing Bubbles ever. Grant is one of the founder members of the ICF, but that's about the least of what he's done; he's practically been involved in, and documented, almost every musical, political and cultural scene around the world. Where the action is where you'll find him. We've gone on to work together on many of projects and you couldn't ask for a better mate than this old school East London international socialist. Daz Emerson and I are psychically joined since Born Slippy, and he's a dyed-in-the-wool 100% Essex boy, and obviously a West Ham fanatic. Back to Cass Pennant: he's gone on to display his entrepreneurial skills as a publisher and filmmaker. A generous a big-hearted friend, it was Cass who helped me get the film of my book Filth made, hooking me up with Jon Baird, who had directed his biopic.

So there have been plenty characters on the terraces and in the stands at West Ham. The one that always got my attention was a guy in the chicken run, whom I never knew to let onto. He stood beside us back the late 70's, early 80's and looked a bit like Prince Charles. He certainly didn't sound like him though:

he was proper old school East End. He specialized in enticing throw-in taking players to turn round, by saying their name repeatedly in an insistent but reasonable, friendly voice: 'John...John...John...' then, if they took the bait and swiveled in acknowledgement or even if they didn't, it would be: YOU FACKIN CUNT! or YOU FARKING NANCY BOY!!

Can't even get away from them in Septic land, as that was where I hooked up with Jason A!

Sometimes you don't choose the good things in life; sometimes they choose you.

There have been frustrations on the way, obviously. West Ham (like Hibs) never enjoyed a fraction of the success they should have, often specializing in spectacular self-sabotage. Both clubs have a history of passing teams off the park and then conceding the softest schoolboy goal. West Ham are currently owned by three of the worst people you could put in charge of a great football club, and have moved from the most atmospheric ground in England to a soulless theme park. Yes, I miss the Boleyn and my seat in the Bobby Moore Upper. It was the place that let me know I was back in town, where West Ham mates would tell other friends I was around. It rooted me and orientated me. Like any metropolis London operates by networks, and if you're a punter, that's mainly football and music. And I've always loved to go out. But I wouldn't have changed my Hammer experience for anything, and I feel very blessed by the connections I've made down the years supporting West Ham.

Thank you Steve, Chris, Phil, Romf, Gutsy, Ivesy, Stuey, Tony, Deb, Grant, Cass, Big Bob, Lager, Kev B, Si, Woody, Jeff, Mulreaney, Steve, Daz, Jase, Lee all those happy hammers that kept me on the West Ham straight and narrow and made sure my aspirations to be a more generic London football fan, picking and choosing my games, was never going to happen. And I'm delighted about that. It was specializing in West Ham that made me feel like a Londoner. That's what football does for you and that's why, despite being Hibs through and through I'll always take an interest in a club in any place I go to live. Bohemians and Ajax fulfilled a similar role for me in my spells in Dublin and Amsterdam. Through working class people at play, you always find the soul of the place you're in. I love art, but the bourgeoisie who limit their cultural lives to restaurants, galleries, theatre's and museums are the ones that are suffering from the real deprivation.

West Ham United: thank you for choosing Welsh.

Pie, Mash and Eels

Pie and mash has been the staple diet of East Londoners for centuries and the London 'pie and mash' shops offer a meal that is embedded in London's history and rooted in the very fabric of London and her occupants. The pie and mash shop was a place you met before your football team played; either home or away. A place you met your mates before a day out and a place you'd taken your girlfriend, fiancée or wife. The working class enjoyed and appreciated the simple timeless and unscripted life qualities that were forced upon us. You'll always remember the food, the family drink up, batman comics, films on the pictures and TV of the day, with radio shows that were still accepted as a form of entertainment and locally held sports teams as well. School days, playground games, conkers and council estate gangs. Family holidays to the English seaside in the proudly owned first car or the train ride with your grandparents for a day out. All as much of many peoples working class upbringing as the local pie and mash shop.

Pie and mash, now accepted as a traditional British corner stone of a cultural identity in many parts of modern London, pie and mash was once referred to as comfort food. Pie and mash remained for decades as a once staple part of a healthy consistent working-class diet and held a common seat at many of London's working-class restaurants originating in the city's East End.

The East End, the 'traditional' area of London, lying east of Shoreditch High Street, Houndsditch, Aldgate High Street, and Tower Bridge Approach. It extends eastward to the River Lea and lies mainly in the Inner London borough of Tower Hamlets, part of the historic county of Middlesex. In the Middle Ages the East End was part of the great parish of Stepney. It began to take on an identity of its own in the 19th century. The area underwent considerable reconstruction following the air raids of World War 2, and with the appeal of cleaner living in neighbouring Essex, overcrowding is no longer a widespread problem.

During the Victorian era, industrial air pollution tended to be worse in the east and south east of London because of the prevailing westerly wind, with the result that the East End was settled more by the working classes, while the western part of the city was home to higher social classes. The working class were poor and favoured foodstuffs that were cheap, in plentiful supply and easy to prepare. The savoury pie had long been a traditional food, and its small hand sized form also made it a transportable meal, protected from dirt by its cold pastry crust, and filled with cheap minced meat, usually mutton. Adding cheap mashed potatoes, together with a sauce made with fish stock and parsley, made it an affordable plate-based sit-down meal.

Pie and mash consists of a minced-beef filling (historically, it was filled with eels, that were in plentiful supply and as an affordable part of the pies ingredients) baked in a pastry crust and served with mashed potatoes and a thin green parsley sauce called liquor (which actually contains no alcohol). Since the 19th century, a common side dish has been jellied eels, and the liquor sauce was traditionally made with the liquid left over from stewing or boiling the eels. Pie-and-mash shops remain popular throughout London, especially in the East End.

Eel Pie Houses, as they were originally known, have been around since the 1700's. Originally, the piemen would carry their pies in trays or small portable ovens to sell them on the streets of London. Early pies were actually filled with eels from the Thames, the eels would have been spiced and stewed in stock prior to being used as a filling. The more successful piemen were able to establish static stalls to increase custom. In later years eels would be replaced with a minced beef meat filling. In modern times the pies are now filled with 100% minced beef.

Jellied eels are often associated with pie and mash, as European eels cooked in gelatine also became a common worker's meal since eels were one of the few forms of fish that could survive in the heavily polluted River Thames. Supply was plentiful through the late 19th century, particularly from the imported fish coming into the London docks via the fishing boats landing catches at Billingsgate Fish Market.

Since 2010, as revealed in a joint study by the Zoological Society of London and the Environment Agency, the number of eels captured in research traps in the River Thames fell from 1,500 in 2005 to 50 in 2010, meaning most eels used in pie and mash shops are now from the Netherlands and Northern Ireland.

The main dish sold is pie and mash, a minced-beef and cold-water-pastry pie served with mashed potato. It is common for most pie makers and servers to present their finished product in an almost ceremonious way - the mashed potato to be spread around one side of the plate and for a type of parsley sauce to be present. This is commonly called eel liquor sauce or simply liquor (the term liquor does not imply alcohol content in its original meaning), traditionally made using the water kept from the preparation of the stewed eels. However, many shops no longer use stewed eel water in their parsley liquor. The sauce traditionally has a green colour, from the parsley. Most pie and mash shops also have a bottle of extra sauce labelled turbo or hot sauce.

Before shops became common, trading took place from carts. It was not until late Victorian times that shops began to appear around working class work-places and living areas. A common argument to this day is, 'who was first?' The first recorded shop was Henry Blanchard's at 101 Union Street in Southwark in 1844 which was described as an "Eel Pie House". The shops have become part of the local community and heritage of their area, for example, L. Manze in Walthamstow became Grade II listed by English Heritage in 2013 due to its architectural and cultural significance.

Traditionally, pie and mash shops have white tile walls with mirrors, and marble floors, tables and work tops, all of which are easy to clean. They give the shops, hardly ever called restaurants, a late Victorian appearance. This by many people's opinion allows a certain value through tradition to be preserved.

A shared city-wide philosophy is when you eat in a traditional London pie and mash shop you are helping to keep alive a London tradition that goes back over 200 years. There are many famous people and celebrities that enjoy pie and mash who make regular visits to their favourite pie shops.

Jellied eels and cockles are other London specialities often sold in pie and mash shops, usually bought ready prepared from wholesalers. Chilli vinegar (vinegar containing pickled chilies), originating from the spice trade imports to the London docks, is also traditionally served with all these dishes. Prior to the introduction of chilies to the vinegar in recent years, the vinegar of choice was a plain malt vinegar like Sarsons.

Pie and mash in the movies

With Mrs. Lovett's struggling pie shop figuring prominently in Sweeney Todd: The Demon Barber of Fleet Street, it seems fitting that a pre-show meal consisting of pie and mash would become a theatre-going tradition. When Sweeney Todd played in London in 2014, and then later in New York City in 2017, audience members would arrive early to enjoy a pre-show experience of indulging in delicious pie and mash

You Never Forget Your First Pie and Mash

Ricky Grover

The first memories that come to mind is my old local pie and mash shop - Lediard's pie and mash on West Ham Lane, which still had sawdust sprinkled over the floor. It was probably from when the old boys used to spit out the eel bones many years before. Also the attraction of your local pie and mash shop was it was just like your mum's cooking. So it doesn't matter wherever you go, it's never really the same as your first pie and mash. Even thinking about the old boy that used to bring out the pies - he was a right big lump, he was always covered in flour, and an old hat and a big hearing aid on the side of his head. Who knows why he went deaf; might have been from the woman serving was always shouting, "more pies!", but It was everything involved, from his actions, his character and the smell of the pies as he brought them out. The thing I remember also is it didn't matter your social class or standing, whether you was tall or short, no one has just one Pie and Mash. Everyone always had at least two, if not three pies. And even then, people would still go up for more. It was more than just a staple part of an East Londoners diet, it was a very addictive food.

Pie and mash was a large part of who you were, as much it really was part of your DNA.

One of the main differences and what was heavily frowned upon by those from abroad and working class from other parts of the country; namely the north, would never accept how Londoners would put liquor on their pie n mash. They honestly thought it was disgusting. To a good few from outside the realms of the M25, liquor was much like a parsley sauce, and to them that was reserved for a fish, not a meat pie. Pie and mash was for a lot of the working class given some times as a reward. So if I trained hard, when I was boxing my idea was if I'd stuck to the training and trained properly, I would reward myself with some pie and mash. Later in life, I'll set goals, and still reward myself with some pie and mash, and that comes from my younger years.

Is there a time and place for pie and mash? Easy - anytime, anyplace and anywhere! Everything changes, Pie and mash then pie and mash now. I don't know what it is and I can't really put my finger on it, but pie and mash back then was much nicer. it could be me getting older, the old taste buds, or it could be that the old spit and sawdust set up was just the real deal. There's a few polymer shops around by me. And they're all good, but for their own reasons. It's like going out for a nice Sunday dinner. One place might have it where the potatoes are just right but the meat is not up to scratch. Then you go to another place and then meat is absolutely perfect, but the potatoes are a bit ropey. So looking back on it all is a good is a few good places, but nothing will ever beat your first place, and that for me will always be Lediards. That place will always be the one in front. The ones from years ago are the ones in front. Pie and mash is definitely a part of my life and will always be. I've brought up my family on pie and mash. Even a different generation within my family identifies with pie and mash - It's who we are. Friends, family, all East Londoner's and they all have pie and mash in their veins and if someone said they didn't like pie and mash, they'd be thought of as a real odd mark. And I'll go as far to say, if someone didn't like pie and mash I wouldn't trust them!

The British Cafe

"Hope is a good breakfast, but it is a bad supper." - Francis Bacon

In Britain a cafe - or respective of your generation or class identity, is sometimes referred to as a working men's cafe, caff or "greasy spoon, is a small family owned, sit-down, no frills, come as you are 'local' eatery. Dating from the early 1800's, the term café came from the French 'café' (meaning 'coffee' or 'coffeehouse') and the Italian 'caffe' (also meaning 'coffee'.) In 1839, 'caféteria' had been coined in American-English from Mexican-Spanish to indicate a coffee-store. But, the cafe wasn't something new as the café has been reborn many times over the years. The years after WW2 left with some, an unwanted lingering air, of as much loss, as accomplishment with those fortune enough to have returned from their dutiful commitment overseas. What was born and a necessary breath of fresh air for those now seeking calm and sanctuary within their home shores, was a new spirit of national confidence in society and family life. This then herald a new era of prosperity within the consumer and members of the middle class. A whole new culture was to be born post WW2, and the birth, or re birth in some eyes of the tea and coffee house goers of the earlier years, was now brushed aside and a new contempory-style, dominated architecture and design of the '50's and the swinging '60's, in not only the modern post war home but also the locally owned cafes and restaurants, was welcomed in.

To many, this new era of wealth and prosperity represented a new vibrancy in society. With advancements in a now modern society, allowed materials like Formica, leatherette chrome and plastic to decorate the cafes of new. This same fresh, clean and modernised appearance and some-what streamlined cult was especially present in the places now to be a multi-generational hang-out. The prosperity and positive age had arrived, the cafes would now reap the rewards of modernisation, a sleek new bold feel and look had taken root to a once otherwise aging industry.

Like most things in life, both history and time has shown us all, the world moves on and nothing lasts forever, as today, you have to look harder than ever to find a real original family owned cafe. The once chalked lettering wall-menu and crested neon or painted lettering sign that read cafe, with their intact with classic fittings, proper seats, and home cooked meals are become less seen. In addition to the ever increasing leases and costs associated with running a traditional cafe in most modern cities, the generation of what was the original Cafe proprietor and owner are sadly in their retirement years, and with their younger siblings and children seeking more lucrative and exotic careers in the modern world the cafe is no longer a common sight.

What can make the cafe a success, is based (on opinion, but not largely refuted and found within all cafes) is as much the food as the friendliness found within. That's not to say, if the food is not up to par, that any decent person will go back for a plate of unfulfilling over-priced food just because the smile and service was good, but the tradition and warmth is a measure of any well- known eatery. The cafe will typically specialise in both home cooked meals and traditional fried food. Though, predating the modern cafe, the same name was a term used for coffee houses and tea shops, they differ largely due to the age of the industrial revolution making eating out more affordable and not restricted to class and wealth.

As a general rule and friendly pointer, never confuse your traditional cafe or caff, with a high street chain restaurant. The unwilling, less than enthusiastic help, listed as staff and the restaurants attempt at a unique experience with their one size fits all identikit deco, gives all the reasons you'd never want to visit an over-priced cold characterless breakfast factory and all the reasons you'd favour going to a multi-generational owned cafe, that offers attention and care to what they do every day off their lives. It's more than your fry-up and cup of tea, here you get glass sugar dispensers with red and brown sauce bottles on laminated tables, the banter, laughing and hustle behind the counter. The clinking of cups and shouting of orders. It's the jets of steam rising from industrial sized, shining chrome tea machines and menus and passed through more hands than a single pound note. It's crowded tables, elbows and conversation. Fluorescent lights and the ringing bell on the busy front door. Its history and families that have frequented the same table and chairs for the last 50 plus years. The food is as important and the people found within. And furthermore, when many people visit somewhere to get something for breakfast, there's nothing less than simplicity as much is there's a person's plan to simply and effortlessly get something to eat and drink. The last thing wanted is the feeling of over thinking and complexity with the new high street branded complexing sanctioned queuing rules and progressive named coffees and size of cup needed.

A British cafe typically offers fried or grilled food such as a full English cooked breakfast, that may contain a combination of ingredients such as fried egg, bacon, hash browns, baked beans, grilled tomato, toast, fried bread, sausages, black pudding and mushrooms. Also, many offer made to order options such as bacon buttys and sausage sandwiches. The main drink served in a cafe is usually tea and coffee, though both soft and carbonated cold drinks are also found on the menu. Coffee is made one of several ways and the type or process varies but is normally instant, sometimes espresso but rarely brewed. Tea, should always be served (when in a sit down setting) in a ceramic cup; as your tea connoisseur will insist that if you're served tea in either a paper or card type cup or something us unholy as a polystyrene cup, you should simply get up and leave. The process for tea is typically brewed and served by a large tea pot. Your 'roadside' cafes; catering to your more 'industrial' type customer, will serve what is known as builder's tea. Builder's tea refers to a strong cup of tea, also known as a builder's brew. This is simply a strong cup of tea that takes its name from the inexpensive tea commonly drunk by laborers, construction and tradesmen on break. A builder's tea is typically brewed in a mug as opposed to loose tea leaves in a teapot.

The Cafe

Carlton Leach

There's few places better for a plate of tradition and a cup of tea than the cafe. The cafe was a staple part of East London's history. To be fair, the cafe was found in most working-class areas. But for me, it was the east London cafe that was the cornerstone and central focal point, where all walks of life would pull in and pull up for a cup of tea and a plate of the best on offer from the menu. It was a place of office staff and dockland workers, who all shared the same space.

There was more than just a community found within and it was more than just the same faces. It was hundreds of years of the same bloodlines, intermingling, talking major local issues such as football and the excuses for the trouble they got themselves in over the weekend. It was the Monday to Friday club for the local working community.

The cafe was a front door to an age-old establishment, a valued place within the community. It was very much part of tradition, no different than supporting your local football team. You knew the owners and they knew you. A place we stopped at before football, always for an away game! Early doors, as we used to call it. Getting your full English and properly topped up, then off to catch the rattler. More so because you knew for your trip up north, you'd be relying on a dodgy meat pie, as your real concentration would be being out on the piss with the lads. So, a visit to the café was a must. That was fuel for the engine. It kept you going.

One thing that is missed is how the café bridges the generations. The grandfather, his son and the youngest in tow. The café had something for everyone visiting. I can't think of anyone that doesn't like a breakfast and what better place than a café, after all everyone has to eat, don't they!

The early cafes had a juke box, all the girls would be there, motorbikes parked outside, occasionally a car, but this was a place that acted as a platform as much as a meeting place for the local youth. For many, the 1960's and '70's cafe held a different meaning and purpose. For the lads, hopefully a chance to pull a bird and for those that already had one in tow, a place to get along, displaying their achievements and egos. But whatever your opinion, whatever your politics, most would learn of a social identity by being part of the café's community.

Everyone from politicians to East End gangsters, your market traders and the young girl on the way to work all visited the cafe. If there's anyone from the 1960's and '70's era that said they never went into a cafe, had never had a full English or sat down for a cup of tea, they were either lying or they weren't in London - and that's a fact!

For me, my memories will always hold firm. Growing up in Canning town, working in the area, the docks and the local cafe. You picked your team colours like you picked your café, but everyone was welcome.

101 commonly used Cockney rhyming slang words and phrases

1. Adam and Eve – believe
2. Alan Whickers – knickers
3. Apples and pears – stairs
4. Artful Dodger – lodger
5. Ascot Races – braces
6. Aunt Joanna – piano
7. Baked Bean – Queen
8. Baker's Dozen – Cousin
9. Ball and Chalk – Walk
10. Barnaby Rudge – Judge
11. Barnet Fair – hair
12. Barney Rubble – trouble
13. Battlecruiser – boozer
14. Bees and honey – money
15. Bird lime – time (in prison)

16. Boat Race – face
17. Bob Hope – soap
18. Bottle and glass – arse
19. Brahms and Liszt – pissed (drunk)
20. Brass Tacks – facts
21. Bread and Cheese – sneeze
22. Bread and Honey – money
23. Bricks and Mortar – daughter
24. Bristol City – breasts
25. Brown Bread – dead
26. Bubble and Squeak – Greek
27. Bubble Bath – Laugh
28. Butcher's hook – a look
29. Chalfont St. Giles – piles
30. Chalk Farm – arm
31. China plate – mate (friend)
32. Cock and Hen – ten
33. Cows and Kisses – Missus (wife)
34. Currant bun – sun (also The Sun, a British newspaper)
35. Custard and jelly – telly (television)
36. Daisy Roots – boots
37. Darby and Joan – moan
38. Dicky bird – word
39. Dicky Dirt – shirt
40. Dinky Doos – shoes

41. Dog and bone – phone
42. Dog's meat – feet [from early 20th c.]
43. Duck and Dive – skive/ hide
44. Duke of Kent – rent
45. Dustbin lid – kid
46. Elephant's Trunk – drunk
47. Fireman's Hose – nose
48. Flowery Dell – cell
49. Frog and Toad – road
50. Gypsy's kiss – piss
51. Half-inch – pinch (to steal)
52. Hampton Wick – prick
53. Hank Marvin – starving
54. Irish pig – wig
55. Isle of Wight – tights
56. Jackanory – story
57. Jack Jones – own
58. Jack 'n Danny - fanny
59. Jam-jar – car
60. Jimmy Riddle – piddle
61. Joanna – piano (pronounced 'pianna' in Cockney)
62. Khyber Pass – arse
63. Kick and Prance – dance
64. Lady Godiva – fiver
65. Laugh n a joke – smoke

66. Lionel Blairs – flares
67. Loaf of Bread – head
68. loop the loop – soup
69. Mickey Bliss – piss
70. Mince Pies – eyes
71. Mork and Mindy – windy'
72. North and south – mouth
73. Orchestra stalls – balls
74. Pat and Mick – sick
75. Peckham Rye – tie
76. Plates of meat – feet
77. Pony and Trap – crap
78. Raspberry ripple – nipple
79. Raspberry tart – fart
80. Roast Pork – fork
81. Rosy Lee – tea (drink)
82. Round the Houses – trousers
83. Rub-a-Dub – pub
84. Ruby Murray – curry
85. Sausage Roll – goal
86. Septic tank – Yank
87. Sherbert (short for sherbert dab) – cab (taxi)
88. Skin and Blister – sister
89. Sky Rocket – pocket
90. Sweeney Todd – flying squad

91. Syrup of figs – wig (sic)
92. Tables and chairs – stairs
93. Tea leaf – thief
94. Tom and Dick – sick
95. Tom tit – shit
96. Tomfoolery – jewellery
97. Tommy Trinder – window
98. Trouble and strife – wife
99. Two and eight – state (of upset)
100. Vera Lynn – gin
101. Whistle and flute – suit (of clothes)

Printed in Great Britain
by Amazon

56863441R00077